The Back Home Series

Series Titles

The In-Between State
Martha Lundin

North Freedom
Carolyn Dallmann

Ohio Apertures
Robert Miltner

Praise for
Martha Lundin

Blending elements of memoir, lyric essay, nature writing, and fractured field guide, Martha Lundin's brilliant new collection accumulates into an incantatory meditation on, and celebration of the queer body, the river's innate meandering, and the sorts of "infinities" that resist the limitations imposed upon them. These essays are full of clear-eyed and intricate declarations of love—for home, for parking lots, for comets and lakes and fish and the Upper Midwest. For bodies bound and unbound. For bodies "that need remembering." Rendered in crisp and sumptuous prose, and grappling toward transcendence, Lundin's work uncovers the beautiful "outliers" lurking amid the ornaments of our world. And in doing so, these essays levitate and whirl, as if miracles.

—Matthew Gavin Frank
author of *Flight of the Diamond Smugglers*

Martha Lundin's *The In-Between State* revolutionizes environmental writing, exploring the fluidity of nature and the natural changeable state of bodies of water, from lakes to humans. These lyric essays pulse with the power of Lundin's imagery and insights about the imposition of borders and the spirit that dares to cross them. This collection marks the arrival of a thrilling new voice in American literature.

—May-lee Chai
author of *Useful Phrases for Immigrants*
American Book Award winner

The In-Between State is about the queerness of bodies, place, and belonging. This is about searching for oneself in the stories we cling to–the ones we attach to neighborhoods, buildings, or trees. Lundin's writing traces Lake Superior and the angles of bodies. Perforating gender into small pockets of the upper-Midwest, they force us into those moments that ping in our chests, those moments we swallow to forget. This is about finding home even when it hurts.

—Zarah Moeggenberg
author of *To Waltz on a Pin*

Thank you for everything! With love,

The In-Between State

Essays by

Martha Lundin

Cornerstone Press
Stevens Point, Wisconsin

Cornerstone Press, Stevens Point, Wisconsin 54481

www.uwsp.edu/cornerstone

Printed in the United States of America by
Point Print and Design Studio, Stevens Point, Wisconsin 54481

Library of Congress Control Number: 2022931843
ISBN: 978-1-7377390-7-4

This is a work of creative nonfiction. All of the events in this book are true to the best of the author's memory. Some names and identifying features have been changed to protect the identity of certain parties. The author in no way represents any company, corporation, or brand, mentioned herein. The views expressed in this memoir are solely those of the author.

Cornerstone Press titles are produced in courses and internships offered by the Department of English at the University of Wisconsin–Stevens Point.

For my parents

Essays

Pulse

River fishing requires a certain amount of tact.

My father is the most graceful when he is on the river, a fish following his fly. He squats, hunches over his fly rod, and slowly drags the leader. His feet move delicately through the current as he tries to find the perfect spot. Something with riffles, tree cover, rocks. He has forty years behind him practicing this art, shown to him by his father. Forty years to master it.

At 21, my grace does not lie in wading through the water, over algae-coated rocks, trying not to trip, or slip, and fall headlong into the tannin-stained river. More often than not I tromp more than walk through the water.

I think, perhaps, the river teaches me how to walk through her body.

When the river floods in 2002, I am 11 and I do not understand the repercussions of such an event. When we make it to the family camp the following spring, everything looks the same. I cannot tell the cabin had three feet of water in it: the floor needed replacing; the stones of the fireplace needed scrubbing to erase the black that stained it. The Escanaba looks the same to me as she always has. My father can tell the difference. Water does not let things stay the same forever, but he memorizes the curves of the river, and the flood carves new canals.

Still, he takes us down the river. I am wearing my brother's too-big, hand-me-down, Sanibel Island t-shirt. It is bright orange, and I like it because it is so long on my 11-year-old torso. There are alligators on it, all green, except for one that's red, their mouths wide open, bearing their sharp teeth. "Dare to be different," it reads.

We do not catch any trout but we manage a few smallmouth bass and a single northern pike. Dad tells us it's good to get the garbage out of the river as he throws the rock bass we catch into the brush on the side. He threads the stringer through the bottom lip of the pike and ties it to the back of the canoe. The fish drags behind us as Dad paddles. He is careful not to take too big of a stroke. I sit on the bucket that has the smallmouth.

On the final leg of the trip, Dad's paddle stroke goes too far back and his pinky catches on the sharp teeth of the pike. Dad doesn't swear in front of us yet, so he says, "Son of a bun!" He rustles through his tackle box, pinky sticking out to the side. A crumpled bandage emerges from the bottom of the bag and he wraps his finger up. By the time we load the canoe and belongings into the back of Grandpa's Chevy pickup, Dad bled through the bandage. Smushed on the bench seat, we spend the car ride back with his pinky wrapped in the orange cotton of my t-shirt. I do not change into a new one when we take pictures.

By the time I am 14, it is clear I do not hold the same passion for trout fishing that my brother does. He ties his own flies: delicate and soft with feathers and beads and tufts of fur. He has his own tackle box. Several of them. A few fishing rods. He is invested in this art. During the summer my father takes this opportunity to teach me a different art:

how to read the river. How to steer efficiently, how to let the water do the work.

I struggle with this last lesson. The current is insistent and pushes the canoe so we float sideways down the wide channel. I want to steer so the bow points downstream. I want to face forward; going sideways feels unbalanced. This seems like it would be the safest option, but Dad tells me it only matters when we get to rougher waters.

He shows me how to predict where eddies will form next to the steep reed banks, how to give low-hanging trees a wide arc to allow for a few good casts into the shadows. He makes sure I know, intimately, the way water flows over rocks, how to avoid the smooth water in rapids. Aim straight. Dig deep.

Two years later, I graduate from steering in the front, to the back. I watch my father cast into the shallow riffles, waiting for that familiar weight on his line: the tug-tug-pull of trout. I guide the canoe down the waterway.

In my family, men are measured by their ability to fish.

To read landscapes, and water temperature.

To look at the surface of the water and name the fly-hatch.

Caddis. Prince Nymph. Blue-Wing Olive. March Brown. Stonefly. Mayfly.

Men are measured by how well they can filet a fish. How cleanly they can cut flesh from ribcage. How quickly they can gut a trout. Men in my family do not wear filet gloves. They need to feel the fish beneath their fingers.

The hands of the men in my family are gentle. When I think of them, I think of the word soft. I think how wielding a filet knife can be a delicate act, instead of a violent one.

Trout do not have scales. They have skin, and a protective layer of slime. They shine in sunlight, gleam of rainbow-speckled silver.

I am 17 when I take my brother's pants from the dryer in the summer and put them on while he teaches tennis. That fall, I buy my first pair of men's jeans. I do not tell my mother. I could not articulate the strength I felt as I pulled them on. More like the armor from my books about lady-knights than denim.

I blush the first time I wear those jeans to school because there is a part of me that thinks I should not want to look like a man. I think I should not feel good in men's clothes. I should not like the way my hips blend away under the loose fabric. I should not like the way the shirts do not pull on my shoulders, do not accentuate my "natural figure." Clothes are such a thin protection.

In my early years at college in the Upper Peninsula of Michigan, I reacquaint myself with the river. It is a long process. My feet do not remember how to slide over the stones and I don't wear waders, opting instead for the comfort of gym shorts. Wearing shorts makes me feel closer to the river, which makes me feel grounded. I like the way the water flows like satin against the backs of my knees—heavy and insistent.

At 19, I keep buying skirts, hoping I will like them. But when I look in the mirror in my dorm room, I feel like I don't belong in the light fabric. For the first few years I was really able to dress myself, I only wanted to wear dresses. Dreamt of pirouetting in pink, tiptoeing in tutus: an illusion of weightlessness. Now, I pull on a dress and I am afraid I will float away. There is not enough weight to keep me on the ground.

So, I pull on two sports bras at a time, listen to my pulse reverberate against the back of my ribcage. Watch the sidewalk as my hiking boots thum-tup against the concrete in time with my heartbeat.

I find it difficult to justify my gender in therapy. The woman looks at me in my first session when I am 20 in the college counseling office and tells me to "pick one." I do not tell her how tempting this is: to follow the line of baggy pants, button-down shirts and ties and wander into injections of testosterone. To shoot "man" into my thigh. To carve the "woman" from my hips. To sharpen jaw, thicken brow.

I do not tell her how much I crave an answer so simple as this. I do not "pick one."

When I am 20, I tell my father I want to learn how to clean fish. He promises.

We float from camp to the Big West. It is seven hours of fishing hard, stopping often. My father says the water is "prime" and we manage to catch our limit. He tells me this is a good sign; the trout population is finally getting back to healthy numbers. The DNR has planted thousands of trout into the river system. We wrap each of our fish in the rough reed grass that grows on the banks, and soak the canvas creel to keep the trout cool.

After the trip, back at camp, Dad takes me down to the river's edge. He holds a trout in one hand, a pocketknife in the other. He puts the knife in the belly of the fish and slides up toward the joining of head to body. I copy him. My trout makes a popping sound as the air exits.

My father shows me how to open the chest cavity, and rip the heart and intestines from the fish. He tells me to tear the gills from the cheeks, and throw all of it into the river. I rinse the fish and watch the brown-tinted water discolor the pink of the flesh as I rub my thumb against the inside of its spine.

I can feel the tiny ridges of the backbone, and the lines of rib that hold flesh to the body. The eyes do not look dead yet. Just very far away.

It is May. I am 21.

Dad and I sit around the fire pit, trout skeletons on our plates. The eyes are white. Not just far away. Dead.

Sometimes I wish myself far away.

My brother sees his sister. But he does not see the sister he grew up with. He looks at my cropped hair, my diminishing articles of "women's" clothes and tells me, "You are still a girl."

He inhabits the binary so securely I cannot tell him it is not so simple as *boy* or *girl*.

When my mother and I look at jewelry she asks if I see anything I like. I lie when I say no. There is a polished gray agate with sterling silver rim but I cannot tell her the weight of a chain around my neck feels like hands.

When she asks if I need a new swimsuit, I point out the one with the highest neckline. I tell her it's because there will be less drag in the water. What I mean to say is that I do not like when there is more than three inches between the base of my throat and the top of the fabric. I want no hint of cleavage.

What I do not tell her is that the reason I have so many sports bras is because I wear two at a time.

What she does not know is that I started binding my breasts when I was 20. That I know the exact angle to hook my finger to pull the bunched-up fabric down my back. That I wait to feel my heartbeat to know I'm still here. What she does not know is that sometimes there are pebbles in my throat instead of words. What she does not know is that the snapping of the Lycra against my ribcage sounds like killing trout.

Outlaw

When I was 15 years old, I applied for the Junior Posse Program. The program was designed to get high school students engaged in local history by having them give tours of the historical society in downtown Northfield, Minnesota. The Northfield Historical Society is located in what used to be the First National Bank and a dry-goods store. In 1876 the notorious James-Younger Gang attempted a bank robbery there.

I knew about the James-Younger Gang long before I was in the Junior Posse Program. Every year in the first week of September, the whole town celebrates The Defeat of Jesse James Days. It's a week-long celebration with carnival rides and reenactments on Division Street. All the locals know that Northfield was the place that stopped the James-Younger Gang. It is a point of pride.

So, when the classes for Junior Posse started, I didn't expect to like the men who came to my town and tried to take everything away. But it got complicated, and I grew a soft spot for the James and Younger brothers.

I feel dizzy trying to understand all the ways I do not love these men. And *but*. *But*. I can't shake a bone-deep connection somewhere to these men. Maybe the connection isn't bone-deep at all—just a shared name: outlaw. Outlaw.

Each truth feels a little bit like a lie.

Before we were allowed in front of guests, the group of students in the Junior Posse Program took a trip to Kearney, Missouri to visit the James' family farm. We had a guide lead us across the property. They showed us where the tree that was used to hang Jesse and Frank's stepfather used to stand; where Jesse was buried—and the headstone that named his murderer "coward." The sun was warm on our heads, and we were all dressed in shorts and t-shirts and tennis shoes. The sky was clear, the grass was green, and as we walked into the house—what today we might call a cabin—in my mind no one said anything.

In remembering my tour through Zerelda James' home, my body thinks *tiptoe*, thinks *she's going to come home any minute and sit in her chair*. Of course, she wasn't. She died in the early 20th century, outliving all but her eldest son.

I was all nerves my first day at the First National Bank. Maybe I called it stage fright, though there was no stage. Only wood floors, and white walls, and printed foam-core board with historical photos. My hands shook and my voice shook and I tried to remember to plant my feet just slightly too far apart so I didn't sway, and I tried to find something to do with my hands.

I greeted guests in the dry-goods store. Some had traveled from across the country—Jesse James enthusiasts—and a few brought their kids. Mostly though, it was middle-aged white couples: the husband in cargo shorts and polo shirt, the wife in a matching linen capris-and-blouse outfit. I never showed the optional video, instead heading straight for the first bulletin board. This is where guests met the James and Younger brothers.

I told them that Jesse James wasn't the leader of the gang. In so many ways, he was just Frank's kid-brother. Frank James and Cole Younger were the real leaders with so much experience as guerrilla fighters in the Civil War.

My favorite photo in the whole museum was a portrait of Frank, Jesse, and Zerelda. The boys stand behind their mother, hands on her shoulders. Zerelda said, "No mother ever had better sons." Looking at her portrait, was there any way to disagree? The whole family looked devoted to each other.

Zerelda was six feet tall, and didn't smile, and I thought about all the loss in her life. What loss creates.

As a tour guide, I wore a period costume. My dress was white with tiny blue flowers all over, lace cuffs, and a high neck. I liked the petticoats on the skirt, how it whispered over the floors—how the whisper contrasted with the thumping of my leather boots on the wood floors. The same wood floors my boys walked over when they came to Northfield.

History as I understood it at 16 was not reality. I could rewrite their narrative in my mind.

Frank James and Cole Younger, the eldest brothers of the gang, served together in one of the most successful guerrilla fighter groups of the Civil War. William Quantrill, the leader of the guerrilla band, taught them tactics. Hitting and leaving was what they learned to be good at. They had an entire war to practice. They mastered thieving.

After the war was over, Cole's brother, Bob, decided they should go north to rob a bank. Bob convinced Jesse, Frank's younger brother. They said they'd do it for the glory of the Confederacy. They'd take back all that stolen

Confederate money sitting in a tiny vault in Middle-of-Nowhere-Minnesota. Tensions remained high on the border between Missouri and Kansas where their families lived. Reconstruction hadn't eased the burden of empty beds. There was no therapy for survivors of war in the 19th century.

They were in their late teens and early 20's when the Civil War ended. Frank and Jesse came home to their mother, sat down to supper with her at the table in front of the stone hearth. They hugged their brother, Archie, shook their stepfather's hand. But they were not content.

I was not content. As a queer high school student, I didn't feel like I fit in. I clung to the other queer students, terrified of losing them when I wasn't yet sure if I would lose my parents when I came out. I felt so far from fitting in, so far from a community, it became easy to feel like an outlaw.

On September 7, 1876 at one o'clock in the afternoon the sun was warm, still more summer than fall. Eight men rode into Northfield, a small, southeastern town in Minnesota. Frank and Jesse James; Cole, Jim, and Bob Younger; Bill Chadwell, Clell Miller, and Charlie Pitts directed their horses across the bridge toward the center of town. Farmers were beginning to harvest the corn crop from fields drying to gold. The bank was ripe for robbing and the men were confident because little Northfield shouldn't have been any more difficult than the train robberies they had been executing as they made their way up through Missouri, into Iowa, and finally through the Minnesota forests, still wild with woodlands and rivers.

Frank and Cole led the heists. But in 1876, they relied on the local, Bill Chadwell, to guide them through the Minnesota country. They had never been farther north than Iowa and their nerves were high.

Travelling attire consisted of a linen duster that nearly reached the ground. Good for hiding pistols. The fabric billowed slightly as the outlaws split up and mapped the town. They pulled the kerchiefs from around their necks. Trousers were tucked into leather boots that had the distinct heel-toe thnck-tik, thnck-tik on the wood boardwalk down Division Street.

When the older men looked at the busy street, they did not feel good about the odds. Townspeople watched the visitors walk past the shops. Nodded to the strangers. Went about their business as the gang scoped out the shops and bank. They were not noticed for their clothes, but for their horses. They were the kind of horses Quantrill taught them to look for. Living in the American Midwest taught them the importance of a horse, and William Quantrill taught them how to pick the best, how to stick a buck, and break out the young ones. Strong and lean Quarter horses: they were the best stolen Union money could buy for the best horsemen Minnesota had seen.

Frank and Cole noticed the eyes on them. There were too many people to ensure a quick getaway. They were all on the street, gathering under the warm September sun. Chadwell assured them the townspeople wouldn't cause any problems. Frank and Cole listened to their younger comrades.

The men let themselves be cocky as they tied their horses to a hitching post and walked to the bar to steady their nerves.

That summer between my fifteenth and sixteenth birthday,s I was wild and unknowing. My hair was still long, and I still loved dresses, but I hadn't told my parents I was queer. I was still trying to figure out what that meant, and what that looked like. I defined myself in the context of my peers but I didn't have idols to dress like. I loved my Historical Society dress precisely because it didn't belong. It belonged to a time that had passed, and so my wearing it was an act of borrowing that era. I loved its buttons and the long sleeves and my boots that sounded like heartbeat. It connected me to Zerelda, and through Zerelda, her boys. My boys. Their histories were drawn, recorded, finished. Mine was only just starting. As a tour guide, I felt like the keeper of their story, and in that, I felt an obligation to portray a side of them the reenactments never did. I could not shake the feeling that these were men who had stories beyond what happened in the years leading up to, and after, the attempted bank raid. *Outlaws*, we named them.

They were brothers, I whispered.

I wondered if the James and Younger boys ever felt different. Not like outlaws. Just outsiders. I began to suspect that maybe their hands shook too when they got into town.

A year before the Northfield bank raid, in January, the boys were out talking about the pros and cons of going north. The Pinkerton detectives came riding through the woods looking for the James sons, on charges of robbery. Zerelda opened the door to the men and shut it, said, *The boys aren't home. Good night.*

The detectives moved around to the back of the house, looked through the waving glass in the windows and watched the woman sit down at the table with her young son. They broke the window when they threw an explosive. It was small and round: rolled into the fireplace where the fuse lit in a bright spark. When it detonated, it threw shrapnel into the woman and child. Archie, eight years old, died in the blast. Zerelda's arm was shredded; a doctor would have come to the house. He would have wrapped a tourniquet at the elbow, amputated her forearm. He probably prescribed morphine and whiskey and clean bandages.

Burn marks scarred the stones of the hearth.

When I thought about that night, I thought Frank would be angry because I believed he was always angry in those years. Frank probably wanted to pluck those Pinkerton fingers off their hands one by one, kneel them on the ground and level his pistol at each of their heads. I imagined Zerelda looked her son in the eye and told him to sit down. I wondered if that's when Frank let his mother see him cry. If he confided his worries about his brother's desire to travel so far from home. If he stared at his mother's truncated arm, told her that Cole's youngest brother Bob was going to Minnesota. They needed to keep Bob and Jesse safe. Asked her why his brothers-in-arms wanted to start another war. I wondered if he told his mother he was tired.

When the gang rode out of the yard early in the morning in the middle of July, I wondered if Frank looked at his mother, told her, *We'll be fine, Ma. See you in a couple months.*

I wondered if she told them not to go.

I wondered if she waved from her porch anyway.

Maybe this was what loss created.

Here's what I told guests when we stepped into the bank: At two o'clock the gang split into three groups. Frank took his brother, Jesse, and Bob Younger into the bank and left the door ajar.

Cole Younger and Clell Miller came in a second group and sat outside the bank entrance, smoking a pipe. Miller closed the door. What they did not know is that people noticed the closed door on a warm September afternoon.

Jim Younger, Charlie Pitts, and Bill Chadwell stationed themselves in the town square, next to the bridge. What they did not know is they would not stay there very long.

There were three men in the bank: the acting cashier, Joseph Lee Heywood; a teller; and a bookkeeper. The bank was laid out simply. It was only a temporary building while the First National Bank was constructed across the street. The counter was open with only a five-foot-tall surround. It was made of cheap pine painted to look like the more expensive oak that would be installed in the permanent bank.

The three men jumped the counter and cornered the teller and bookkeeper farthest from the vault. Jesse watched the men while Bob searched for any money in the drawers. Frank pointed a gun to Heywood's head, "Open the vault." The clock read 2:01.

Heywood did not open the vault. Frank dragged him to the door, and told him, again, to open the heavy door, with painted flowers. Again, Heywood refused. Forgetting himself, Frank took the butt of his revolver and knocked the cashier unconscious.

Outside, J. S. Allen tried to go into the bank, and was blocked by Miller. When Allen saw the gun the outlaw was carrying he ran down the street, shouting, "Get your guns, boys! They're robbing the bank!"

Allen handed guns and ammunition from his hardware store to anyone who could shoot. The robbers fired shots into the air to try and keep the streets clear, but it didn't help. Townspeople were not only shooting at them, they were also throwing rocks and other debris. Women were not cowering inside storefronts. Men did not flee. They were part of a town still trying to make it; they would not give up so easily.

Cole looked toward the bank doors and wondered what was taking so long.

Jim, Charlie, and Bill joined in the fighting on the street. Clell Miller was lying dead on the gravel, a lead ball shot through his subclavian artery and lodged in his shoulder blade and soon Bill Chadwell joined him, shot through the heart, dead before his body hit the dirt.

Cole ran to the doors of the bank. He pounded on them, looked over his shoulder, "Get out here, they're shooting our men."

Things were not looking good inside.

In the bag that was supposed to hold the contents of the vault, was the small sum of twenty-six dollars and seventy cents. Frank was angry.

Heywood was regaining consciousness. Frank heard Cole, and as Heywood leaned against a small table, Frank leveled his gun and shot Heywood in the head.

The three men exited the First National Bank to see two dead men and a dead horse. They tried to clear the streets of people, but it didn't work. With a shot kneecap, Frank mounted one of his horses, and the rest of the gang did the same.

Before they left, Cole noticed they were missing someone. Bob, with a shattered elbow, and a shot in the leg, couldn't get on a horse. Cole leaned down from his saddle and hoisted his brother up behind him.

The men cut the telegraph lines on the way out of town. It was 2:07 in the afternoon.

What they did not know was the vault was unlocked the whole time.

At 16, I spent a lot of time thinking about all the ways the heist went wrong. Comical, almost. How, at every turn, they made the wrong choice.

I knew it was not wrong to be queer. But that didn't stop me from running through all the ways in which the world called me wrong. Called queer a choice—a wrong choice. Was loving my boys also a wrong choice? Wouldn't it have been easier to side with my town?

When I led the guests out of the bank and into another room, this was what I told them:

The bank robbers split up. Frank and Jesse headed west, while Cole took his brothers and Charlie Pitts and, together, they headed south. None of them were doing well. Cole, tied to his horse, was falling in and out of consciousness from the blood-loss caused by eleven gunshot wounds. Bob's elbow was gangrening.

The men wrapped their wounds the best they could.

They incited the largest manhunt in history. Two thousand men were searching for them; the boys did not have the luxury of stopping. They were 384 miles from home.

Cole, Jim, Bob, and Charlie were cornered in a swamp exactly two weeks after the raid. Charlie Pitts was killed in the shootout and the men who brought the Younger brothers to the Stillwater Jail were named "The Magnificent Seven."

At 16, I did not like The Magnificent Seven. They were no different, to me, than the boys. The Magnificent Seven cornered the gang in a swamp and shot them for the sake of a sack of money. It is better to love my boys.

I kept coming back to the shootout on Division Street. Kept thinking how men who learned to shoot during the Civil War shot to hit—to kill. But that day on Division, no one on the street died because of a bullet from the gang's guns. My 16-year-old self refused to believe that was a coincidence. And I won't argue with that logic now.

With his gunshot wounds treated, Cole sat in front of the sheriff. He was given a pencil and a small slip of paper. *Who else was in the gang?* the sheriff asked.

I imagine Cole in an uncomfortable chair, wounds swollen and patched. I imagine he looked at the sheriff, chuckled, just once, and wrote his statement: "Be true to your friends if the heavens fall." He scrawled it—there was no hesitation in the lines. It was the only answer to the question.

On slow afternoons I paced through the museum, listening to the thnk-tik, thnk-tik of my boots. I imagined Cole beside me, imagined Frank next to Cole playfully shoving one another—schoolboys always, though they were probably never that in life. I imagined Cole pointing to his signed statement to the sheriff, and telling me about his family. Saw Frank and Cole in my mind's eye clearly: men who would lose everything except for one another in the aftermath of that piece of paper.

The Younger brothers were sentenced to 25 years in prison. In prison, Bob was an accomplished woodworker. But soon he lost his appetite and he sweat through the night, and he didn't have enough energy to lay the mother of pearl into the wood. And then the cough came. *Consumption*, they called it—an engulfing kind of death. His lungs did their best to expel the bacteria that lodged in the walls, slowly consuming the muscle, working to consume his whole body. At first it was just phlegm, but soon it turned to blood, and soon his lungs didn't cough, and soon his lungs didn't do anything at all.

Jim, after serving his twenty-five year sentence, stayed in Minnesota. He fell in love with a reporter. But the state denied him a marriage license and he became depressed. In the middle of October, 1902, he took a pistol to his room at the Reardon Hotel in St. Paul and put the barrel to his head—a different kind of consumption.

Frank and Jesse escaped the authorities. Jesse, true to form, attempted to create another gang but it was never as successful as his brother's. After a few robberies, one of his members, Bob Ford, came up behind him in Zerelda's home and shot Jesse in the back. She was making breakfast when she heard the shot.

Zerelda buried her son an extra three feet down in her front yard. She carved into his tombstone, "Murdered by a traitor and a coward whose name is not worthy to appear here." She covered the plot in stones from the creek her sons played in. For twenty-five cents, visitors could take a rock from the grave. She replaced the pebbles each morning. She watched from her porch.

I pause. I picture her sitting there. In my mind, she has a rocking chair and she dresses all in black. I imagine she never leaves her mourning attire. I think about everything and everyone who was taken from her. How she had to bury her son further away from the surface so no one dug him up. What must that weight have felt like?

After Cole's release with his brother in 1901 he promised the state of Minnesota to never come back. He travelled home to Missouri where he and Frank founded the *Cole Younger and Frank James Wild West Show*. Together they went on the circuit lecturing about their life of crime. They died a year apart in Missouri.

Outlaws.

Brothers.

Outlaw is a name given and taken and owned and warped and bent until it belongs only to the self and no one else. It is a name kept safe and redefined. At 17, I abandoned dresses and traded them for heavy pants, and heavier boots, and baggy shirts. At 20, I began binding my breasts. I thought about pebbles and dirt sitting on my chest. But I finally felt like I wasn't buried. I learned a new word: genderqueer. And I knew exactly what that meant without having to be told. It evoked the feeling of living outside a prescribed binary. An outsider. An outlaw. The name felt like a new kind of clothing. Something I had always been looking for, but couldn't find. I hadn't been looking in the right place.

With a new language, I found it possible to talk about my body the way I had always been able to talk about the boys: with a certainty that there was more than outward appearance to us. There is a wide, deep stream. An unlocked vault.

How to Look

When I was 24, I picked up one of my pads of paper, a handheld mirror I stole from my mother when I was still in high school, and a pencil and eraser.

I sat down and I looked at my face.

It felt like I was relearning my body.

Art used to be magic. In high school I learned how to see—really see—something. I didn't just look at an object. I looked at every line, every shadow, every color that made up those shadows. Suddenly, all my classes were excuses to figure out how lines went together. How lines created bodies, created movement, created the illusion of light.

I loved drawing and the way the graphite smudged my whole hand because blending was easier with my fingertip than with a blending stump. I loved watercolor: the way paint seeped into the ridges of the paper. How I could put clean water down first and then watch the paint spread. Watercolor was soft in ways that acrylic and oil paints were not. I liked that I could choose how much control I had over the art.

In high school I fell in love with the lines of ballerinas' bodies. Not because the body was necessarily supposed to move that way, but because it was capable of moving that way. Within the art, I learned their bodies through mathematics—used trigonometry to describe their angles.

I printed out photo after photo on the family computer, and put my ruler to the paper. I extended the lines of their body, tried to figure out how the angles were made. Saw how the arms were parallel to legs, asymptote perpendicular to head and toes; or how arms elongated the line of their chest cavity, an extension of their spine. The bodies felt like infinities.

At six, I wanted to be a ballerina. I wanted to be what the world told me a ballerina should be.

After avoiding it for years, at 25, I looked at myself in the full-length mirror hanging on the back of my closet door, and I tried to find the lines of my body that I did not hate. I stood and looked at my legs. I cocked my hip and memorized the curve of my waist, how my breasts lay on my chest. I called them breasts, and I reminded myself breasts were not inherently womanly. I couldn't believe I had to remind myself of such a thing—that I needed the reminder in the first place. I looked at my belly button, a tiny oval in the middle of a stomach that on bad days was the ugliest part of me, and on good days was just another part of me, and I tried to remind myself it was good enough.

Art lost its magic in college. I left the art major in my second year of college when I was 20 years old. I did not like how sticky the oil paint was or how the canvas seemed to reject the pigment. I didn't like how my brush pushed the paint around. In high school I painted with watercolors and the pigment soaked into the stretched paper and it was my job to save the highlights on the paper because there was no "white" paint.

When I dropped my major, my painting class was in the middle of a project. The professor assigned us a still life of cardboard boxes. We sat with our canvases and stared at those brown boxes. I hated it. I didn't want to paint boxes. The boxes didn't make me feel anything. I could not figure out how to make cardboard magic.

When I left the studio major in college, I think my mother saw, more than anyone, how much it hurt me to give it up. She told me that I was not allowed to stop making art.

I promised, but it has been a hard one to keep.

The longer I stay away from it, the more I forget how to see.

I searched for words to define myself. In high school I clung to lesbian. Four years later, it was no longer enough. I came to genderqueer and held onto it as tightly as I could, but I did not love my body. There was language—definition—but I couldn't look at myself in a mirror. I stopped drawing portraits. I stopped painting. I packed everything away, and told myself I'd get to it later.

I took a trigonometry course in my third year of college. I spent most of my classes doodling in my notebook. I was bored, and when I was bored, I drew naked women. Breasts and hips and thighs filled the margins while sine and cosine and tangent wiggled in the space adjacent. Sine and cosine were my favorite to graph because they stretched out over the x-axis in balanced waves that were predictable. They couldn't shift in shape halfway to infinity. This was comforting to me.

There were limitations even for infinities.

There were an infinite number of equations to modify sine and cosine waves. But once the equation was set, in theory, the wave would just go and go and go until it hit something.

This, too, was comforting: knowing that I, too, would always run into something. There was always going to be an ending point to whatever track I was on. And then maybe there would be new coefficients and this would metaphorically start me toward a new infinity.

I try to remind myself I am good enough.
My body is good enough.
It becomes a mantra: *enough, enough, enough, enough.*

When I was 17 and art was still magic, I had to mimic an Impressionist-era painter for my Drawing and Painting class. I loved ballerinas, so I chose Degas. Of his nearly 1,200 paintings, dancers make up almost half of Degas's work. He painted them in rehearsal spaces—while they were tying their shoes, stretching, talking to one another. Always together with other dancers, other musicians.

I learned Edgar Degas hated painting ballerinas.

Degas loved light. I love lines. I love angles—how bodies interact with themselves.

Somehow, in loving angles, I forgot how to love my body.

I saw myself as a body without sharp lines: no clear clavicles, no arrow of ribcage, shoulder blades barely visible, soft jaw. How did I forget that no body is sharp? That is an illusion.

Rembrandt painted more than 90 self-portraits between the start of his career in the 1620s until his death in 1669. A visual autobiography. One of my art teachers in high school told us we'd always have something to draw, because we'd always have ourselves.

It follows then that the curve of my hip, the shadow at the small of my back, the softness of my body should be something of a comfort to me. It is mine. It is the only body I have, and I am trying to control the way my pigment sinks in, while still leaving spaces of untouched paper. The transition of self belongs to no one else.

But, in this one instance, I would prefer my body to be average. Average would feel so much more secure. I would fit neatly under the bell curve. Sixty-six percent of the population would be there with me, and despite my introversion, I think that's comforting.

My body is an outlier.

The queer body is an outlier.

And queer people spend hours trying to manipulate their bodies so we look like we fit within the bulge of the bell curve.

I'm trying to make my body fit. Fit into clothes, fit on a piece of paper, fit into a label. Having a body that can be defined and recognized in a category is comforting, if limiting. I want to want to transcend the boundaries of labels and the categorization of queer bodies and sexualities, of art and mathematics, but I'm not there yet.

In my room at 24, I sketched out my eyes first. These, I love. It is the softness of the skin—how this is a softness I allow myself—the shadows right under the lid, the crease above the lid, the way the light reflects on the iris—a bright highlight in the black of the shadow and pupil.

When I reached the line of my forehead, I thought I must have gotten it from my father. The winter after I dropped my art major, I started calling myself Matthew. My queer identity was shifting and I looked for something to hold on to. I held on to a forehead that felt distinctly masculine in a body that felt too feminine to call "he." I got my eyebrows from my mother. Feathered on the ends, these, too, in their scrappy, unkempt way, were evidence I could have passed if I wanted to. At 20, this mattered.

The glasses that framed my face were, in some ways, the most masculine thing I owned. It was the square shape, the dark red, the thick lines. These were not delicate wire, curved oval, or light green.

My hair was the shortest it had ever been, clipped close to my scalp. It was my hairline, not my hair, that squared my features, and this was what I wanted.

My nose is straight, the cupid's bow of my lips, pronounced. When I was drawing portraits more often, I started at the lips, and worked my way toward the eyes. My teachers told me I was going backwards—I should draw the head shape first, then the details; but I wanted to give the faces voices first, then sight. I checked in on the paper to make sure the corner of my mouth lined up with the center of my eye.

I needed to know I was seeing myself for who I was, instead of who I imagined I was.

It was about understanding.

It was about understanding my body instead of ignoring it. When I was 20, I could not fit into any sort of prescribed bubble. I bound my breasts, changed my name, gave myself new pronouns. I was trans, but I did not want to transition. This was a hard line to straddle. A complicated one. I unchanged my name, kept my feminine pronouns, kept my binder.

Ballet used to be a parlor trick. Just wires attached to the heels of slippers and ladies held up by the tension. But then those women realized they could train their bodies to do what wires had previously done so that when Degas came to the dance studio, he could paint the process of readying. The satin, tutus, tights, paint, jewelry. It is the light in the paintings that make it look like it's being seen through gauze. Like it's still some sort of magic.

There's a large part of me that believes I would find clothes that fit—to fit the identity that is mine—if I lost x-amount of pounds. The number doesn't really matter. If I lost however much weight I determined was the right amount of weight to lose, there would be more options. Less fat to fit over.

I would have hard angles, sharp lines. This would mean I was trans enough. But I've lost track of how I came to the conclusion that being "trans enough" meant being sharp.

It all comes back to lines.

I joined a gym to try to change what my body looks like. And then I will have to relearn my body again and again. Over and over. More infinities.

Asked to explain trigonometry now, I would be able to outline, roughly, the basics of how to calculate sine. I could sketch out the graph: start at zero, a curve moving like a wave cresting at 1, troughing at -1 and ending back at zero after a period of 2π. It is only a hazy recognition that this is important, but why and for what purposes, I couldn't say. The period has something to do with a circle, but trigonometry deals primarily with triangles. It is lost to me now four years later, how these shapes intersected—sharp triangles and soft circles.

In my trigonometry course in college, I bought gridded notebooks to keep my notes and graphs tidy. It was a habit I picked up in high school for my statistics class. I did not like the look of bell curves on lined paper—it was a matter of preference, aesthetic. It was satisfying to see how tidy my notes were. Satisfying to see the order.

There was a lot of pleasure in the precision of graph after graph of sine, cosine, and tangent curves. With the addition of a single coefficient, the graph could be stretched vertically or horizontally, like taffy.

I bought a gridded notebook so I didn't have to carry a ruler to make sure all the graphs were set up exactly the same; I could see exactly how the coefficients changed the shape of the curves.

When I stood back from my self-portrait, I scribbled one last shadow at the corner of my nose. It looked like me, but not like me. A measurement was off, something gone awry. My face looked too wide, my mouth too firmly set in its frown. I was glaring out of the paper. I must have noticed this while drawing, but I did nothing to manipulate my reflection in the mirror.

The other option, of course, was that it did look like me. That was what I looked like. It was not my drawing skills that went rusty. I spent so much time not seeing myself that I no longer recognized my face sketched out on a piece of paper.

Hanging over my bed is an ink drawing of a kingfisher, with a dragonfly in its mouth. I completed it during my freshman year of college in Drawing 101, when art was still magic.

I can still see the pencil grid on the paper. It came out of a sketch pad. The paper, by design, was thin with little tooth to it. It made it ideal for ink, but less so for graphite. Because the paper had no bite to it, it was hard to get a wide gradient within the image and harder still to erase whatever lines I put on the page. I never could erase the grid lines. Dealing with the black ink and the white of the paper was easier. Every line had to be deliberate.

We, as students, were always instructed to grid the paper first.

The grid allowed me to focus on a small portion of the photograph without getting distracted or overwhelmed by the whole. I had to go square by square, unintimidated by the 86 squares if I was only focusing on one of them.

I remember the squares being massive. Three times the size of the source image. If I tried to draw that kingfisher now, six years later, I doubt whether I could. The image would inevitably be distorted the same way my self-portrait was.

It may be time to start gridding my paper again.

The Violence of Comets

I found the rooms between the violence of comets.
I threw myself into anything's path.
–Jeremy Radin

When I am 19, a woman shoves her hand down my pants in a parking lot and I let her. The yellow lamplight casts deep shadows on her eyes and a bright highlight—halo—at the crown of her head.

Later, after we are dating, I let her undress me and my hands tremble because I do not consider myself desirable. She lays me down on her white shag rug and her hair tickles my cheek. I feel ugly, but I do not tell her that. *Scary Movie*'s credits roll.

After, she asks if I am okay. I smile and say yes.

I let her undress me when I do not want her to.

She pushes. I close my eyes. I think I am supposed to let this happen.

When I am 19, I leave her, and she tells me I am ugly. I believe her. She walks out of my dorm room, slams the door behind her. Comes back a few minutes later. I have learned to expect this.

She tells me I am not allowed to be sad. I believe her.

She tells me she is going to kill herself. I believe her when she tells me this would be my fault.

I have nightmares about her coming through locked doors.

An asteroid is an inactive body orbiting the sun.

The word originated in the early 19th century from the Greek word meaning "star-like."

But they are not stars.

I have a one-night stand with a woman after watching *Hook*. She undresses me on her bed: shirt, pants, bra, and underwear, until I am only wearing socks. I do not undress her. I do not pull her to me, but I kiss her and she tells me I am beautiful. I do not believe her. Maybe I say thank you. She pushes. I let her. At this point I do not think I am allowed to tell her no.

I lie awake next to her while she snores and her cat's bell jingles in the hallway.

The next morning, she drives me to campus and the woman who comes to me in nightmares sends me a text message, calls me "slut." I do not thank the woman for the ride back to my dorm.

Comets also orbit the sun, but they develop tails of dust and gas as they approach the sun.

Asteroids and comets, when far away from the sun, are difficult to tell apart. They are practically the same thing.

Still, they are not stars.

When I am 20, I sit in the room of a boy with a bottle of vodka.

He gets drunk mixing it with root beer and tries to unbutton my jeans. I push him away. He kisses my jaw and I try not to think about the alcohol on his breath.

He says he loves me when he's sober and my hands tremble because I believe him. And I believe him again when he tells me I am beautiful. It is his conviction as he says it. It is the blue of his eyes.

He holds me when the nightmares come; when my eyes go away mid-thrust, he stops and holds my face, tells me to look at him. He tells me to name him. To recognize him as not her. He does not push. And I think about safety, and that for the first time in a year the nightmares stop for three weeks.

He leaves in March. He does not come back. He says I shouldn't have expected him to stay. I think I deserve this.

A meteoroid is a small particle broken off from an asteroid orbiting the sun.

Most of these burn up when they enter the Earth's atmosphere.

The nightmares come back.

In the dream she walks in and tells me I asked for this. Like I invited her through the door. Sometimes she presses on my thighs where I used razor blades to draw lines and her hands are on fire and she looks at me with cold eyes. I cannot move. I do not scream. She does not leave.

I wake up sweaty. I check the deadbolt on my door. Unlock it. Lock it again. Go back to sleep.

When I am 21, I undress a woman, and feel her pulse under my lips. She does not undress me, does not reach for me, kisses me anyway. It isn't until a year later that I think about how familiar that sounds.

When I am 22, I wonder if she wanted those nights. When I ask her, she does not tell me. She does not talk to me for eight months after I ask her. I assume the worst. When we talk again, she does not bring it up. Neither do I.

A meteor is what we see as meteoroids burn up in the atmosphere. They are tails of light streaming across the sky and disappearing.

We call them shooting stars, but this isn't accurate either.

When I am 22, I trace spirals on the torso of my lover. I tug his boxer briefs so that I can see the skin of his hipbones, soft points in the light of the lamp. I learn his body differently, and he learns mine differently. We do not ask to be naked in front of each other.

We try to relearn what it means to see. Try to relearn the definition of a body.

On a morning in June, we wake up together and I go to make coffee. He tells me I was crying in my sleep. He didn't know if he should have woken me up.

I tell him that next time he can wake me up.

Our unsteady hands hold each other and we are something whole for a summer.

A meteorite is a body that survives its passage through the Earth's atmosphere. It makes landfall, falls into the ocean, or nestles itself deep into dirt. Some are large enough to create craters, but most, by the time they reach land, aren't much bigger than a small rock.

When I am 23, I press my palms to a woman's hips, breathe into her belly button.

I drink wine and hope she does not see my hands tremble.

On a morning in June, we wake up together and she goes to make coffee. When she comes back, she tells me I was crying. She asks me about the nightmare.

I tell her it's the same as always: a door opening and shutting.

She doesn't ask any more questions.

There are nights when I hold her face, and I name her over and over again and she looks at me, afraid of the fear in my face. She does not ask what I see. She does not want to know, and I can tell because it's in the way she nods along to my anxious rambling. How she is far away too. Maybe with someone else.

She does not hold me if I do not ask her. I want her to want to hold me. I want to be held together by someone else's hands. When she leaves me, I think it is my body's fault even when she tells me it's not.

Asteroids can have erratic orbits. Scientists track their trajectory by predicting where they will be and recording when and where they actually show up. It is inexact: guess work until enough data is collected.

When I am 24, I get drunk on whiskey and thread my fingers through a woman's hair and kiss her. I breathe into her jaw and the hollow below her ear. We are drunk on all the ways we hate our bodies, and all the ways we do not hate each other's bodies.

She likes rough hands, and I like my hands on her stomach, and her throat. I like her arched back and the way my hands twist around her hair. I like my hips on top of her hips.

She rolls me over, kisses my neck. I think of the boy with vodka, and the woman in my nightmares and I push her away. My hands shake. She notices. She asks if I am okay. I say yes. I mean no. I close my eyes. I shake my head. I can't tell. I feel reckless.

I leave another bruise below her collarbone.

I want her to hold me, but I don't let her and I don't know why that is. I watch my hands shake and I squeeze them into fists. Squeeze so tight until my knuckles are the white of full moons, and crescents carve themselves into the meat of my palms.

She says it's okay. Everything is okay. But I feel far away from her and my body and even though there are moons in my hands, I can't come back, even to them.

I am afraid I am turning into someone who pushes. Who leaves. I wonder if I use alcohol the way the boy did: to hide the way my hands shake; to pretend that they don't. If I let my hands tremble their way to hips and belly buttons and clavicles and jawlines then there is something—someone—to hold on to, and I can ignore the face from the parking lot stuck in the middle of my forehead. If I leave bruises in the shapes of asteroids on clavicles because I want to claim a body and leave it marked then everyone will know I am not in control, I cannot be trusted. If I press my thumb against the throat of a lover the way the boy with vodka did, then no one will try to hurt me. If I crash into enough bodies, maybe I will be able to redefine what it means to leave. If I collect enough data on myself, maybe I'll be able to predict my own orbit.

I think of meteorites. How scientists do not have to guess at their location, because meteorites can be found. They can be held. I think about how they were first an asteroid, and then a meteoroid, and then a meteor, and finally, at reaching the ground, they find a final name: meteorites.

I think about the ground and the way meteorites can damage the Earth, but rarely so much that the land cannot repair itself. Rarely so much that the meteorite cannot become a part of the land. There are asteroids that exist that could destroy everything, but they are so many miles and years and galaxies away that I have no way of imagining a reality where that asteroid becomes meteorite.

I think about my hands. How, when they shake, I grab for something solid. Ground myself. Even if that grounding is just myself. I am learning to define myself as solid. In these people I wanted to call celestial, I was looking not for an orbit, but a resting place.

Picnic

I meet Lake Superior when I am ten. My father takes my brother and me to Picnic Rocks in Marquette, Michigan, and I haul my new snorkel set, bulky and awkward and bright pink, under my arms. Dad carries the towels; Peter has his own snorkel mask and fins. They fit a bit nicer in the security of his lanky limbs. We set up camp in the warm sand thirty yards down the beach from the car, lay our towels and sandals on the slow slope.

The rocks that give the beach its name sit in the water: a set of three black boulders, lichen-covered and seagull-festooned. "1986" is painted in red and white on the largest of the rocks for the high school reunion. I love the rocks because they are black, because they are named Picnic, because they have been colored in paint and droppings and moss.

"It's going to be cold," Dad calls to us as we rush toward the blue.

We run in anyway. When our legs hit the water and the cold, we try to stop but the lake trips our feet and we fall in.

Lake Superior closes over my head only briefly before I kick up from the sand-bottom. My mouth grabs at the air but my lungs won't inhale. Peter is next to me, hair spiky with water.

Dad wades in more cautiously. Knowingly. "You guys okay?"

My breath back, I say, "Yep."

Later, while Dad takes a break on the beach to read his Newsweek, Peter and I take our snorkel sets to the water's edge. There is a rock-bed in about eight and a half feet of water. We are going hunting.

A book back at the rental house describes all the different types of rocks found in the lake. Peter is looking for agates, fools' gold, conglomerates that are not concrete chunks. These are considered rare. I find I like sandstone best. Sandstone has been compressed under the weight of water and waves. There is a lot of sand, so there is a lot of sandstone, but I don't mind that my rocks are common. I like that I can feel the granules. On land I trace the striations of color around the body of the stones: rust and eggplant and squash. They are not always round, but they are always soft-edged: they take on the shape of the cliffs, of the boulders called Picnic, of the waves that rolled them. Hard and soft all at once.

We return to this beach the next year when I am 11. Dad says we should swim out to the black rocks. We leave our snorkel masks and fins on our towels.

Peter does not like the deep water, does not like swimming in lakes. There is no control out here. But we go together anyway, headed toward the middle of the three. Dad never takes us to the far-left rock. Peter and I don't question this decision.

We are only about ten yards away when I accidentally look down into the water.

"Daddy?"

"Yeah?"

"How much water are we swimming in?" Usually when I ask this question, Dad sinks down to the bottom and estimates the depth based on how long it takes to touch. But he doesn't do that this time. He just looks down too.

"Thirty feet? Maybe a bit more?"

"How come I can see the bottom?" Below my feet, the lake floor is no longer sand. Replacing it are very large rocks, some the size of kayaks and ship anchors. They are all washed-out blues and greens and grays. Some of them look purple. They are all smooth and hard, without the fuzzy look that algae lends. Rocks are not as beautiful when I cannot hold them in my hand, worry myself over the curves of their creation.

It feels like looking over a cliff, suspended above the ground, floating on blue like some sort of cartoon. The mind only sees the distance to fall. Gravity doesn't read.

I am frozen there, treading water, imagining my feet caught in one of the crags, unable to get it out. Stuck at the bottom of the lake.

"We have to keep moving, Martha." Peter has already reached the rocks, anxiety propelling him in the direction of something solid.

"I'm scared."

"We'll swim on our backs for a while. How does that sound?" I do not hear the urgency in my father's voice, but when I am older and know about the way water steals warmth, I will understand his desire to reach my brother.

"Okay." I turn over and look up at the blue of the sky, feel my father swim next to me. My breathing slows as the lake buoys me up.

We reach the boulders with no other hiccups, and clamber up the slope, picking our way around the seagull droppings. The rocks are hot from the sun soaking into the black pores and our bare soles, in their discomfort, are short-strided. We reach the top of the first boulder and collectively stare over the edge. The water is 15 feet below us, ripple-surfaced. I don't see the soft current moving out. When I am 11, there may not be any current at all, just water burbling against tiny islands. Quiet, still, and steady.

There is a ledge that is a little closer to the water and we scoot down on our butts. It is just like a diving board, I keep telling myself. But the sight of the boulders 50 feet down has me frozen again. Peter jumps in first. Heights do not frighten him. This kind of water is not scary to him. If he can see the bottom and know it is deeper than he can touch, and if he can see that nothing will grab him, then the lake is nothing but adventure.

Dad jumps in ahead of me, like we used to do when I was really little at the community pool. He would jump in first, and then tread water to the side of the diving board and wait for me to jump in. A safety net. I did not need him, but it was nice to know he was there.

I leap off the side, convinced by the heat of the rocks and the coaxing of my father and brother. The lake catches me. When I come up for air, Peter and Dad are waiting, and we swim the short distance to the next rock, which is much the same as the first, though bigger, and there are more seagulls squawking at us. Dad calls them rats with wings. But I like how sleek and clean they look: white-chested, gray-winged, black-and-yellow beaked. I think they are not so bad. Common, like my sandstone.

We walk across the ridge on the top of the boulder. When we reach the spot just above the red and white numbers, we make our way down off the rock, slide into the water, and swim back to the shallows.

In this moment, I am not afraid of the lake. I love the water more than I have ever loved anything. Lake Superior is big and cold and I lend her pronouns because she feels so alive to me. So permanent. And I think she will always be there to catch me.

She catches me when I am 12, and 13, and 14. And she catches me and my father again when I am 17 and we swim out to the reef just behind Picnic Rocks and perch ourselves on a submerged ledge.

I am changing. Everything is in flux, and my dad and I talk about the tennis season, and ACTs, and where I want to go to college, and what I'm going to study, but I do not tell him how nervous I am to be considering studio art for a major, or how nervous I am to be gay and going to college because what if I make the wrong choice. I do not tell my dad that, at 17, I don't really talk about the gay thing because I haven't learned how yet. We just leave it to the ether. I give all my anxiety to the lake because she is a good listener and she is so large and has so much space to hold my worries. They are only a drop to her.

I end up going to college by the lake. In August, my parents drop me off at school. The summer is a warm one for the Upper Peninsula, and Dad and I go swimming once before my parents head back to Minnesota and leave me to settle into college life. We head to a different beach at Presque Isle, but the lake is the same here as she is at Picnic. The water is cold like I remember and the true blue of Crayola markers, and I look down wonderingly at the boulders below my feet and they are not scary anymore. She feels the same as she has always felt, and I am glad for this small piece of home.

In the first three weeks of the semester, four people drown. Three were swimming toward the reef behind Picnic Rocks where Dad and I were two years before. The wind was probably up. Little waves probably licked the students' faces. Insistent. They may have tried to swim around the back of the biggest rock. But maybe the rocks were too slick to clamber up. Maybe the water pushed too hard and flushed them back toward the smaller boulders. Maybe their arms grew tired of fighting against the water and getting nowhere and maybe the cold seeped into their skin and there was no one to call to for help.

Warning flags in red mark the beach, but I keep swimming there because I know every inch of that stretch of sand and water. I have memorized the rock bed 20 feet out and where to build the best sandcastles and the way the beach is striped in sections of pebbles and sand and how in the middle of summer it is striped in a rainbow of beach towels and plastic coolers. This beach is more home than my dorm room. I tell myself I am not like those swimmers who went out late at night when the beaches were closed. I tell myself I'm not like those swimmers because I know dark water is so much harder to read. I love the lake and I know not to take advantage of her kindness. I tell myself this as if the lake can know this also. But she can't.

When I go swimming at Picnic on the last nice day of September in my freshman year, I float on my back, staring at the blue of the sky and the white puffy clouds. I like that I am back at the beach that feels so familiar. I want to call it mine. I am surprised when I stand up, realize I am pushed in line with the far-left boulder, the boulder we never went to as kids. We never swam in this part of the beach. I am closer to the parking lot than I am to my towel.

It is such a small thing—to be pushed so far off track. Doubts work like that, though: wheedle their way in and set up camp. I do not know how the lake could have changed. It feels like betrayal. Like too much change all at once: lake and school and strangers that are also my friends. I stare at the clear, glinting water lapping at my knees and walk out of the lake and I remember all those times my brother and I went body surfing. And though my mother never went to the beach with us, she was adamant we didn't go any deeper than our knees so that when the waves washed back, our feet wouldn't pull out from under us. She said something about rip currents then, and all I knew about them was that you had to swim parallel to shore and just keep swimming until you reached land or someone came to get you. But I learned that while watching the Discovery Channel. Mom always made sure Dad watched us when Peter and I went swimming in the waves to make sure we didn't go too far out. Standing on shore, looking out at the rocks feels a little bit like the lake has become a stranger too. Or a friend I no longer recognize.

Picnic is closed to the public by the following year. Four people get stranded on the rocks, and the Coast Guard has to rescue them.

Cards are printed, emails are sent around to the campus population, posters are plastered on every bulletin board, lamp post, and free wall. Freshman orientation classes talk about respecting the lake. How it isn't safe to swim at night, or during storms. There is so much we can't see below the surface of the water.

The postcard that lands in all our mailboxes shows an aerial photograph of the water at Picnic Rocks: navy and speckled white caps. There is no writing on the front of the card. None is needed. The white caps act as arrows and they rush out through the same channel that Peter, Dad, and I jumped into, and swam through, and climbed out of. Beyond the channel is nothing. Only miles and miles of water. HOW TO SWIM OUT OF A RIPTIDE is printed on the back.

I find new beaches to call home. Relearn Lake Superior's body and my body and try to find the middle ground in all of it. But in the middle of a lake, there is no solid ground: only shit-covered boulders that in the heat of summer are slope-slicked with algae.

My mouth stumbles while talking about my body. I cling to "genderqueer" and bind my breasts, hoping to feel some sort of relief. It feels like rip currents, the way I rush away from myself. Over the course of six months, I have two names and three different pronouns. And I research testosterone injections and talk to trans men about their transitions and can they still sing, and do they ever feel like something is missing. They all tell me the same thing: I am more myself now than I ever was pre-transition. But I am not sure that I feel that way. I cling to the label of trans the way I cling to the familiarity of the lake.

The lake's sand is cold more often than it is warm, and I spend a lot of time sitting on the shore looking out over the still waters late in the evening. Lake Superior doesn't do anything for the convenience of anyone else. She swallows ships and people and land, and I accept every part of her.

And I try to take note of the way she does not apologize for other people's ignorance. She does not move out of anyone's way. She is permanent in a way that my gender is not. She is cold always but freezes over less than once every 15 years. I am trying not to freeze myself over. I don't yet know how to be soft and hard at the same time. But Lake Superior is patient and she will wait for me.

Directions Home

Despite making two trips to the Upper Peninsula every year from the time I was an infant until going off to college, when I had to make the trip for the first time by myself for winter break, I emailed my mother in a panic, "Will you send me the driving directions from Marquette to Northfield?"

Terrified of getting lost, I printed out the step-by-step instructions and followed them, checking every five miles or so to make sure I hadn't missed a turn. My father would have said something like, "Just make sure you're heading south and west. You know the way."

I made my mother print off the directions from Northfield to Marquette when I made the return trip too. Each time I emailed her a little more embarrassed that I hadn't memorized the route yet, or simply kept the sheet of paper in my glove compartment. When I graduated three years later, I found that I had kept them: six copies crumpled up in my trunk, under the passenger seat, in the glove box.

After about the third trip, I knew I did not need the directions. But they made me feel safe.

I met him on the first day of February. It was a leap year. I was in my second year of college. We hung out in the study lounge of my dorm, taking black Sharpies to the bodies of fluorescent yellow and green t-shirts from Wal-Mart.

He wrote a quote about perseverance, or overcoming, or winning. The handwriting was neat, exact, sitting perfectly centered between his shoulder blades.

I drew a portrait of a woman I didn't know in the corner of my shirt's torso. He asked to keep it. I didn't even hesitate. What would I have done with a safety-green cotton t-shirt? And he was so beautiful with his swooped hair and blue eyes and strong shoulders.

He pulled the shirt on over his white undershirt. I liked seeing something I had made on him; admired by him. I liked seeing his arm caress the woman's cheek. Imagined it was my cheek. Shook my head to get rid of the image. Someone who looked like him would never go for someone who looked like me. His body was all angles and straight lines. Mine was not, and I had just read somewhere that people are attracted to partners of equivalent beauty. When I looked in the mirror, I found myself to be ugly because I defined my body as opposite to his, and thus, opposite to beautiful.

I noticed his wrists. His knuckles. Delicately bony. He had figured out his place in the gender binary, while I was still muddling through the middle and when I thought of the word masculine I could only think of sharp lines. When I looked down at my knuckles, the bones of my hands seemed to me more dimple than defined.

I was never good at memorizing exit numbers. But, by my third year at college, I could have listed off the way each turn looked: whether there were hardwoods or scrubby pine trees; if there was a median on the road; what the speed limit was, and where troopers were posted to catch speeding drivers.

The Elk Mound exit comes just after mile marker 50. A sharp clover-leaf curve seems to erase the trees as the highway opens up to development. From there it's 108 miles of six-lane to Wausau, Wisconsin—the halfway point to Marquette, Michigan.

The next day a group of us gathered in his room, and he got drunk on Absolut Vodka and A&W Root Beer. We shoved the two twin beds together to accommodate the four of us in a single puddle of blankets and bodies.

At some point the A&W ran out, and he started taking swigs of vodka straight from the bottle and I watched, clutching my cardboard cup of water, sipping. I was not yet 21, and didn't feel like getting drunk.

Our two friends passed out somewhere around one a.m. wrapped in each other's arms.

I know the most efficient way to get through Rhinelander, Wisconsin. There are three stoplights and then a left turn opposite the tractor dealer, and then three more stoplights. On the right between the second and third stoplights is a school, and immediately after that a YMCA, and the lawn with the royal blue hodag statue.

I can name the only church on the side of the road in Sugar Camp, Wisconsin because of the statue of Saint Kunegunda. She is the patron saint of fishermen. And then, just after, the White Stag Bar's whitewashed elk statue bugles silently at passing vehicles.

We stayed up talking, his speech slurred and sloppy. His fingers tried to fumble the button of my jeans open and I pushed his hand away gently. He mumbled something about my body and "attractive" and "touch" and even though I was flustered because I couldn't recall a moment anyone had actually called me attractive; I did not know him and he was drunk. He apologized and I said it was okay, because I wanted him to like me.

The alcohol leaded his eyelids and he fell asleep soon after, nestled in the crook of my shoulder, and I stared at the ceiling of his room, listened to the slow breathing on the bed. Thought about the way a year ago I would have let him finish unbuttoning my jeans. Would have let him do whatever the alcohol told him to because being considered attractive was enough of a reason to let someone fuck me.

In my last year of making the trip from Minnesota to the Yoop, I started taking a back road, Highway 55, and I turned up the radio so the bass thrummed in my chest and I drove too fast over the hills, pushing 75 miles per hour on the straightaways, slowing down only for the tight curves. The road signs to the right of me showed black right-angle arrows with "25 mph" printed beneath. In the fall I watched the leaves blow and settle in my rearview mirror. I knew cops didn't patrol a road that didn't get used.

At the junction of 55 and 2, I passed someone else's Lundin Boulevard, turned right onto Highway 2, and drove through Iron River.

In the morning, sober, he apologized again. We ate breakfast in the dining hall across from his dorm and he sat next to me and let his leg touch mine. Later I asked him if he meant what he had said.

"Of course. Why would I lie?"

That was enough of a reason for me and I ignored the girlfriend, or ex-girlfriend living downstate because he said he broke things off and why would he lie about that?

It was 28 days to spring break and somehow we attached ourselves and I did not talk to anybody for four weeks except him, and we stayed up into the early hours of the morning and I fell asleep in my Romantic British Literature class and blamed it on my professor's soothing voice, instead of the two hours of sleep I got. I went from his room, to class, and back to his room, and some days I did not leave his room at all. I called him safe.

In the middle of the month, I read *Anthem* by Ayn Rand out loud to him. He fell asleep halfway through but I kept telling it to him, in case he woke up from dreams of lanterns and tunnels and marching people.

There was an anxiety I could not define to get every detail of him committed to memory.

From the stone church in Iron River, it is 15 miles to Crystal Falls. I came out of the forest, down a hill, and met two gas stations, a Subway, and climbed back up another hill to a flashing yellow light. I turned right, and then left at the flashing red light; coasted down the hill past the bowling alley, movie theatre, antique stores, and the pasty shop. In the middle of the bridge over the Paint River, I checked the water to report back to Dad. It's low always except in May. Once I was over the bridge, I passed the cemetery and one patrolman and then I was back in tree cover.

I mapped the details of his room: black Coffee Mate with stale, molding coffee; Folgers French Roast; bulk powder creamer; disposable insulated coffee cups; a mini fridge filled with half-finished bottles of water; white towels; Paul Mitchell shampoo and conditioner; Crest 3D White toothpaste; deep red bed sheets on one mattress and gray on the other; navy blue comforter; flat screen 20-inch television; Clorox wet wipes; overflowing trash can.

I mapped the contents of his wardrobe: Old Spice Champion; cologne from American Eagle; black sports bras before he traded them for a binder; American Eagle boxer briefs in hot pink, and patterns of fluorescent silhouette eagles; Aeropostale low rise stonewash jeans; white Hanes undershirts; plaid button ups in blues and greens; mismatched socks; skater shoes.

The stretch from Crystal Falls to Sagola is the longest twelve miles of the trip. Miles and minutes stretch. At Sagola, the junction of M95 meant I was securely in the Upper Peninsula. Even though the land did not really look different from the previous 60 miles of Yooperland, it was a switch that flipped as I watched the odometer tick away mile by mile, waiting for the train tracks and the flashing red light and the BP gas station and the logging trucks that turned right toward Kingsford.

I did not spend a night away from him. Time passed too quickly, or maybe it slowed down. Sometimes, when I remembered that month, it felt like both at once.

Three weeks in, he slid his hand up and around my throat, squeezed, and I pushed him away and stared at him, surprised. Thought about the woman who shoved my legs apart a year before. Thought about the man who did the same to him. It felt violent instead of affectionate.

"I just wanted to," he told me. And I tried to tell him it caught me off guard. He apologized, and I said it was fine, because I did not want him to leave. But it was not fine and my hand stayed fastened to my neck's pulse. Minutes contracted into seconds. Not safe. He threw the t-shirt to me. Told me I could get dressed. I did, and then I walked through the snow back to my dorm room.

I turned left at the flashing light, passed fields and wetlands, and craggy rocks and stubby long-needle pine trees. There were rickety barns and barbed-wire fences that never seemed to be holding anything in. Maybe they were there to keep deer out.

Channing has an old train station and a bar and a single pump gas station with a Pepsi-Cola sign above a Pabst Blue Ribbon Beer ad.

Republic comes up after the Moose Crossing Next 10 Miles sign.

Ten miles to the junction of 41. I turned right, followed the signs for Ishpeming, Negaunee, Marquette. Home.

I watched him drive away in his silver Ford Focus on the last day of February out of the parking lot of his residence hall. I said, "I'll see you when you get back." He mumbled something like, "Okay."

He did not text me that whole week. When he came back, I visited him in his room, kissed him, and he said he was back with his girlfriend.

"You shouldn't have expected me to stay," he said. "You knew this was temporary."

The first time I missed a turn I was flying down Highway 139, past harvested farm fields, golden in the autumn light. The road spat me out at Highway 8 next to a biker bar called Mudslingers and no cell service and I had to follow the signs toward town names I recognized. I couldn't believe I missed my exit. I felt so turned around. I had trusted my ability to always find my way home. But I hadn't even seen the sign.

When I reached Crandon, I called my mother and confirmed that I would indeed run into Highway 51 from 8.

"Where is your atlas?"

"It's in my apartment. I didn't think I would need it. Please check?"

"Okay. I'll call you back. Love you."

"Thanks, Momma." She did call back. 8 would run into 51. I just had to keep driving.

By the time I missed that turn, he had already dropped out of college, moved back downstate, got hired to work at Chrysler, and started T. When I saw him six months after that missed turn, in a Dunkin' Donuts outside Detroit, I barely recognized him. A missed turn. I couldn't find my way back to him—realized he hadn't ever been Home. Wasn't the safe place to rest I had wanted him to be.

When I drive away from the parking lot, I race north back to my lake, back to Marquette. I listen as my wheels hum over the Mackinac Bridge. Blue stretches out in each direction. And then, forest. Two-lane back roads. Railroad tracks and rivers. All flowing, it seemed, back home.

The In-Between State

My father's family comes from the Upper Peninsula of Michigan. They come from rivers and Great Lakes and cedar swamps. They come from quilted flannel, chooks, and deerskin choppers. From aluminum canoes and hardwood paddles. From DIY downriggers and three-horse motors.

They come from six-month winters. From owning three different types of shovels, at least one of which is located in the trunk with an extra set of boots, mittens, and blankets. But they know that anybody who says there are only two beautiful months doesn't understand the first warm day of March comes like an exhalation of winter. In June the mornings are cool, holding on to the last drops of snow. In September, the northern lights spread across the sky like blue and green chandeliers. And anybody who says leaves in autumn are just dying haven't seen the waves of rust, copper, and gold lick tree boughs as they fall and puddle. They haven't seen the moon rise full and orange over Lake Superior in October. My father's family knows that each season is just a different ocean.

They come from walleye, brook trout, pike, and perch.

They come from too many cans of PBR, and cigarettes.

I become most myself in the Upper Peninsula, on the Escanaba River. I learn to read the river like a book and know the difference between safe water and smooth, and

I never had to read Hiawatha to know where to cross her bed of limestone. She is hard-bottomed, and in May she is hardheaded as she swallows the snow that melts into her belly, and she runs fast and clear down.

Water knows how to flow in only one direction: downhill. It takes the path of least resistance, and then almost spontaneously carves itself a new destination. A teacher once said "spontaneous" is just the scientific word for "magic."

It is instinctive to lend water femininity. Lend, like she doesn't deserve to own it. I know water in ways I do not know how to be feminine. The Escanaba River taught me everything I ever needed to know except how to be a woman.

When I am 22, I move to North Carolina in, locals tell me, the hottest month. When I visited in June, the Spanish moss seemed to float from the trees. Delicate. Lacy. In August it looks like the moss drags itself from the branches, pulls against the confines. Maybe that's just me. Maybe I'm pulling, or being pulled. I can't see the moon from my apartment. It is hidden behind a group of trees and condos. If I maneuver to just the right angle down by the retention pond, I can catch a glimpse of it. But only if the summer rains do not cloud the sky.

I try to understand why I get so turned around in my first few weeks on campus. There's something about trees that are all the same height, and no hills—no vantage point—no way to gain my bearings. I find I wander the city in the same way I wander the university campus: in circles.

My uncle builds a cabin on the river's shores when I am 10, but it doesn't weather the way a cabin should. It stays bright and brassy. Before he builds, he clears the cedar and fills in the boggy swamp with gravel. I learn creation is nothing more than upheaval.

The year the cabin is completed, my father takes me and my brother to the river's edge. "We're going to build a riffle." There's not enough movement on the surface of the water to hold trout.

My 10-year-old self and my older brother wade upstream in our swimsuits, shoving our limbs through the current to find the right-sized rocks. Mostly these are just rocks we can easily carry back down to where my father is digging out a trench about five feet wide. Beneath the layer of sand is thick-packed clay, stained orange with iron. His shovel hits the clay, sinks in slowly as the earth softens.

After an hour, and a divot in the riverbed hollowed out, we stack up the collected stones and create an artificial wall just upstream from where we launch the canoe. The water trickles through and around and over the stones. My brother and I find sand and pebbles to pack into the spaces, and some of it falls through to land in the eddied water below the rocks. Dad says, "Looks good." He knows what brook trout like more than just about anyone, and he says they like a soft-sand bottom to rest in.

Peter and I go swimming after our hard work. We try to swim upstream, windmill our arms as fast as we can, open our eyes into the current. The water is tea-colored and a little foggy in the middle of summer. No matter how hard we try, the river always pushes us downstream, slowly and surely and lightly, until we set our tennis-shoed feet down into the rocks and stand up smiling, a little out of breath, and let the water run around our knees.

That night we sit around a hissing fire of green logs and listen to gurgling water at the bottom of the hill. Above us a moon hangs in the sky and I have never seen so many stars all at once.

Behind my apartment in North Carolina, we have a retention pond. As far as retention ponds go it isn't the ugliest: angular with algae blooming to the surface; some dead, dried cattails. I watched a snake eat a frog one afternoon—black ribbon launching into muddy water. On hot days the pond smells like something died, but I am homesick for fresh water and I spend long hours on my porch drinking coffee and watching the turtles sun themselves.

There is a little blue heron that stalks along the edge of the pond. He moves so slowly in the water his steps create no ripples, and I tell myself to take note. I shave my legs and underarms. I take out my makeup and replace my dried-up mascara and sharpen my eyeliner. I'm trying to blend in the way the heron does. If I make no waves, I will be safe.

I thought moving to a city would give me anonymity. There is too much space in the Upper Peninsula to be nobody. But at least in all that space there are people who wear flannel and baggy jeans and hiking boots to church and I am not so alone. At least I did not feel like I stood out.

When I am 11, the river floods.

The snow washed into her during a thunderstorm and she rose. And she rose. She covered her banks and seeped under the tobacco-colored cabin, and she rose. She pushed her way through the floor, over the river-rock fireplace and then she labeled it hers: stained it earth-gray, and settled into the creases. When she finally receded, she took nothing with her, but left her gray silt.

When we take our trip downstream the next year, my dad is sure something is off. "The river looks different." He rounds a bend and I do not know what he means. I could have sworn the birch tree leaning over the water was there last year; I snagged my lure in it in an overzealous cast toward the far shore. I remember because we lost the lure and Dad said, "Next time, flick."

"There's a deadhead that's moved." And I wonder how he can know this: 40 years fishing a river does not make one an expert on where fallen trunks lie. But he is adamant: there was a tree, it was underwater, it did hold trout, and now we have to keep moving. In the canoe, I don't think about how fast and how high the river has to be to pick up and carry a sunken tree.

Within my first week of arriving in Wilmington, I fling myself into social outings including some weird, awkward dates. I do not know how to go about these things, or if there's a proper protocol for clarifying one's needs for friends so I ask one woman if she would like to grab drinks. We do. We throw darts in the dark of a bar called Blue Post with her friend, and I end up winning by some great miracle, though I have a feeling it has something to do with the PBR in her hand, and another in his. We get along well enough but she never tells me her name, or I couldn't hear it over the din of the bar and so she just remained an anonymous thread of text on my phone.

A week later, she sends me a message saying something like, "There's a band playing downtown, you wanna come?" And I say sure despite the fact that I hate large crowds, because I am trying to put my best foot forward, be a good sport, get out of my comfort zone.

I park a few blocks away, near a church. The trees that shade the street have roots that boil up from the ground. I try to remind myself that back in Michigan, I'd find this beautiful.

As I turn down Market Street, I pass a few bars and a few more men in white t-shirts, baseballs caps, sinking shorts, and leather flip-flops. They congregate outside party buses smoking cigarettes. I pass by one as he spits his chew. I tell myself he is not aiming for me. The police are not swarming the street because men spit chew near the feet of queers. They are out to make sure no one drives home drunk. And I am not drunk. Do not plan on getting drunk. I don't want the attention of the police or men outside party buses. They make me equally nervous for different reasons.

My phone buzzes with a text message alerting me that she has moved out of the crowd and closer to the Venus flytrap sculpture, and I see her, staring at her phone, perched on the steps of the boardwalk.

"Hey. How are you?"

She tells me, "I realized I hate Bon Jovi."

"It could be worse?" I don't like Bon Jovi either.

"Yeah. I suppose it could. They're almost done." It's clear they are. They're playing "Livin' on a Prayer" loudly and the crowd is swaying and singing along badly like Bon Jovi fans do. A few of them may have been waving their beer cans or lighters. It's hard to tell when they're all swaying out of time with the music.

We hit a lull in the conversation, and I take the opportunity to go to the bathroom. The women's room is occupied and I lean against the wall an appropriate distance away from the boyfriend who is obviously waiting for his girlfriend. A man walks up to me, "Hey man, you waiting for the restroom?"

"Oh, no, I'm—" and I point awkwardly at the other door. He looks at me.

The door to the restroom opens, and as the girlfriend exits, I duck into the quiet humming of the yellow fluorescent light.

When I get back, she is standing. "What should we do?"

I have no idea what is available at 11 o'clock at night that doesn't include a bar, but I look at the water over her shoulder, and the moon above the battleship and say, "Wanna walk the river?" She nods and we head downstream.

The boardwalk thuds hollow beneath our shoes. As we pass the pavilion, a man sitting at a small table yells, "I know I see a couple gays." She keeps her head down, hands in pockets and I copy her, listen to my pulse throb in my ear, concentrate on the lapping of water against wood. We do not say anything to each other. We move a little bit farther apart and do not make eye contact with the man in the white tank and cut-off shorts. I realize this is the first time I have been yelled at by a stranger for being queer. I feel blindsided by my surprise. Hate exists everywhere. Difference is dangerous. And I stand out.

I notice things like how the "bad part of town" also happens to be where a lot of people of color live, how the woman next to me on the boardwalk is a person of color, how she doesn't talk about that, how she doesn't even live in Wilmington. I notice the Confederate flags in front of houses, and statues and commemorations to Civil War generals. I try to understand this as a nod to history, but I can't help but feel uncomfortable when there is no remorse in the glorification of those men in power.

I notice that people tell me they want to live downtown. Downtown: where the houses have "character." Downtown: where the Bellamy mansion proudly proclaims the house was built by "free and enslaved black artisans." I think about how often I hear rhetoric that proclaims enslaved people loved their slaveholders.

I notice people's noses turn up slightly when I tell them I like living in midtown. I can see their minds spin: *But you're not close to anything.*

The river is the most familiar thing I have here but it smells different. Like dead fish and motor oil. Cape Fear is wide in Wilmington as it prepares to empty itself into the Atlantic. It is tidal and brackish, and so, really, it is nothing like my river in Michigan. Signs litter warnings on the boardwalk: *Submerged pilings, no diving; Strong current, swimming prohibited.* The signs do not say anything about the large amount of boat traffic.

"You're used to fresh water, aren't you?"

"Yeah, I haven't quite gotten used to this place."

"You will." She sounds so certain.

But I wonder if getting used to the air, heavy with humidity and salt, will happen in the same way that I have had to get used to standing out. She tells me to pick something to do the next time we hang out. But I don't. And I don't text her again. And eventually I delete the conversation thread from my phone. Maybe we both stood out too much.

I think, *This is where I live.*

The cabin has a shower but it is generally understood that when the air is warm enough, we bathe in the river. I remember the way the water seeped into my hair, softened it. Conditioned my skin.

After a month of settling in, a friend and I venture to the beach. The ocean beckons: big sky and big water and big sand. In my backpack I carry a towel, a bottle of water, and sunscreen for my paling skin. Under my arm is a folding chair.

Nestled between motels and private homes, the public access point opens itself to sand. The air is salty with sweat and ocean-breath. The sand is striped in fine granules and chunks of broken seashells. It is stubborn like glitter and sticks to my newly-shaved legs. We walk about 100 yards down from the entrance and set up between a group of college students who had a cooler, red Solo cups, and a large tiki-straw umbrella. I don't see things like this up north either and I wonder why towels aren't good enough.

She unfolds a sheet that belonged to her mother in the sixties and we spread it over the sand, plop onto the cotton, slather more sunscreen on our skin.

"Did you want to go swimming?" I nod. "I'll meet you in the water," she tells me and I walk to the ocean. It's been years since I've gone swimming in water really warm enough to call warm, and I don't waste any time jumping into the waves.

The water stings my eyes, drips from my lips onto my tongue. I turn around and she smiles at me as she wades in.

"It's so salty." I'm not sure why I feel surprised, but I lick my lips again and again.

"Oh, yeah. You only swim in fresh water."

"Doesn't the salt hurt your eyes with your contacts?"

She tells me, "Not anymore. I'm just used to it."

There is something white in the water, and the nearest thing I can think to compare it to is a birch branch and I move to try and grab it. But then the surface of the water flutters and it is clear that it is not a tree branch, but a fish, and the animal swims away from my predator-hand. After appropriately overreacting to a live-something in the water near my hand, another school of silverfish flutters by. I reach in again, and watch the fish swerve around my fingers. It feels like magic.

"You don't understand. Fish don't come near people in the U.P.," I say as a way of explaining why I am still squealing over the third school of silverfish to pass us.

When I tell her I thought it was a tree branch, she looks at me surprised. "Why would a birch branch be in the ocean?" And as I look at the shore lined with beach houses and grass, I realize there aren't even scrub oaks around here. I feel foolish. How could I have forgotten so fully that I am not home?

Sufficiently pruny, we slosh our way out of the surf to dry off on our beach chairs. My hair feels coarse as I run a comb through it: the way it felt when I went swimming in a stream with too much iron. The bristles almost squeak as they pull out the small catches. Iron, salt. Different minerals doing the same work.

"We live here." And I say this as I try to encompass two miles of beach between large piers, water that fades from turquoise to deep blue, and a sky that is blue on the horizon. Behind us thunderclouds begin their daily rumbling. I say this to remind myself that it is possible to love parts of this place.

The Escanaba River flows quiet and slow in the fall. The leaves color her surface and puddle in the eddies. She is patient in autumn; her belly is flat. The cold calms her and she looks clear as glass. There is so little water and we bring grouse breasts to her shore, rinse the sticky feathers from the meat in the current and she turns our hands pink. The trout have moved to deeper holes, readying themselves for the long winter. In the cold months, the warm water settles near the bottom of the river, instead of the top where ice forms.

My roommate and I drive to the beach one October evening in our first semester of graduate school. The sun has set and the clouds have moved off. We leave everything in the car, walk barefoot towards the sound of waves.

We settle down in the damp sand away from the water. Heat lightning illuminates clouds on the horizon: great billowing mountains of water vapor. They have not moved to cover the moon yet, waxing to full, three halos crowning its face.

My roommate turns to me, says, "I miss seeing the moon."

"Me too."

He says, "We live here."

And I think, Yes.

And I think I don't yet know what that means. I do not know how to live in this place of salt air and big water that doesn't act like my water. A place of scrubby trees, and asphalt. I do not yet know how to live in a place where forests do not thrive, where huge trees are cut down for the sake of a new apartment complex. I do not yet know how to trust the ocean. I live here becomes a mantra to see all the beautiful things in this place where the air feels suffocating in its heavy humidity. But I am not suffocating.

Ode to a Dead Puffer Fish

You said, "When you write about our breakup, don't forget the puffer fish."

But before this, so much.

First, silverfish in the ocean.

First, quiet evenings in your living room, bedroom, kitchen.

First, cooking meals and drinking wine. Washing dishes side by side. Me, washing. You, drying. Indie music streams from your phone. I think this could be for always.

I think you taste like the ocean and I think if I have you as a home, I can make the ocean home, too.

First, *I feel so loved.*

Then, fleas in your apartment. Chemical burns on your feet and hands. Flea bites on your ankles. They will scar.

Then, staying at my place because you couldn't live at yours.

Then, a new apartment you hate. The smell of glue and new linoleum stuck in your nostrils. But you make a home out of it. I want to believe we could make a home out of us.

And I repeat over and over, *I want to marry you.* I do not say this out loud. But I think it with my whole being.

Then, Thanksgiving.

Then, "I don't want to be together anymore. I felt alone the whole day. Have felt alone for months." I did not know.

And I feel like a fool.

Now, the puffer fish.

I cannot forget.

I am in the middle of a sentence when you run towards the carcass. I follow you—always followed you. The beak is half-buried in the sand. Fins and tail stick up. Most of the skin has shriveled. But the spikes flare out—still trying to protect itself.

You tell me to include the puffer fish when I write about you. You presume I will write about you. You are right. And I will include the puffer fish. Because it is dead and still working so hard not to be soft—not to show how much it hurts to be soft.

Litany of the Saints

When I was 20 and a sophomore in college, I sang in a Catholic church choir, not because I was Catholic but because my mother's best friend was the director. She and her housemate were in charge of most of the music at St. Michael's Parish.

I liked that it was called a parish. It seemed like a small, and, therefore, friendly community.

And because I had been watching ghost-hunting shows that dealt with exorcisms, I liked that the church was named for the archangel Michael, one of God's most trusted angels. It was Michael's sword that cast Lucifer out of heaven.

It was Michael that created the binary of heaven and hell.

My paternal grandmother is a devout Catholic. She converted when she married my grandfather, and since leaving the Lutheran tradition has never strayed from Church Doctrine.

Some stories say Lucifer loved God too much. But I think Lucifer loved God the way my grandmother loves the organ.

She went to college for a degree in music. Piano. She learned how to play the organ while she was in Duluth, and came back to Escanaba, Michigan to settle down. She settled down with a husband and five kids and a growing piano studio. On Sundays she played for mass.

When Dad, Peter, and I visited my grandparents in Escanaba, I was Grandma's shadow. I went to church on Saturday mornings to watch my grandmother practice for mass the next day. The rose window in St. Pat's Church had a stained-glass depiction of Saint Cecilia, the patron saint of church musicians. When I was young, I thought she was judging me from her window because I had a hard time sitting still in the pew in the balcony while dust floated in the air.

My favorite thing to do when Grandma practiced was watch her feet dance over the pedals. I loved her special organ-playing shoes: they were black and shiny with a tiny heel, and had a buckle like my Sunday shoes. I loved how she didn't even have to look at her feet or her hands. When I took piano lessons back in Minnesota, my teacher sometimes put a book over my hands so I had to look at the music instead of the piano keys. But Grandma knew all the notes, even the ones under her toes. Sometimes she let me sit next to her.

On the songs I knew, she let me sing along.

In between each piece, she swung her legs around and stood to face the pulpit below her, acknowledging the pauses that would happen on Sunday.

It was at St. Pat's that I learned to love a church best when it was empty.

In college, I learned quickly that Holy Week was sort of a big deal in the Catholic Church. Much bigger than services surrounding the Easter of my childhood in Minnesota. St. Mike's had a mass every day of the week leading up to Easter morning. On Easter there were five masses.

As a part of the choir, I was expected to attend these services.

Lent has always been my favorite church season. The music is quiet and contemplative, and written in minor keys. The songs feel more like treading water than drowning. More like chanting. It is not the bright and brassy celebration of Easter and Christmas.

Growing up in southern Minnesota, I attended St. John's Lutheran Church with my dad and brother. Each year, on the Sunday before Lent began, the Sunday School classes buried canisters with slips of paper printed with "Alleluia" on them in the courtyard, and on Easter Sunday, unearthed the canister to mark the celebration of Jesus' resurrection. All the children yelled, "Alleluia! Alleluia! Jesus is risen!" We knew the words. We had a vague idea of what it meant. But it was the digging up and opening of a jar that made Easter Sunday special.

I found myself hoping the kids of St. Mike's got to unearth their Alleluias, despite knowing the ground was frozen solid under three feet of snow.

When my grandmother was the organist for St. Pat's, she played for eight masses between Tenebrae on Wednesday of Holy Week and the last Easter mass on Sunday.

I am not Catholic. Lutherans don't have saints. I was told to pray to God. I learned about patron saints when I sang at St. Mike's. There is a patron saint for pretty much everybody and all the confirmands had to choose a patron saint to be named after at the Easter Vigil service.

Six days before my twelfth birthday, I took communion in a Catholic mass for the first time because it was my grandfather's funeral. After Grandpa died, we stopped going to Escanaba to visit Grandma. Instead, we met at my uncle's cabin to go trout fishing.

When I was 15, I learned that my grandmother cried because my family and I took communion. My dad, brother, grandmother, and I were at camp, and the boys were going on a float trip, and I was heading to church with Grandma at the local parish. She reminded my dad that I was not allowed to take communion, because I had not been confirmed in the Catholic church.

There was a lot of yelling, and a lot of "it doesn't matter" on the part of my father, and a lot of "you don't understand" on the part of my grandmother, and I sat on the edge of the porch feeling guilty for eating a communion wafer when I was 11.

I learned my grandmother went to confession on behalf of my transgression against the Church.

If I repented and converted to Catholicism, I could have the whole host of heaven and all God's saints to call upon.

It feels a little extreme. A little elitist.

I would not tell my grandmother this, now. She was happy I was singing in a choir. She was happier it was a Catholic choir. The name mattered, though I never understood why.

At 20, I joked I was earning my place in heaven by participating in Holy Week. There was a part of me that hoped it was true. That if in fact an infallible God made me flawed, then spending ten hours over four days in mass as part of a religious tradition I did not grow up participating in, nor was welcome in, would earn me my place in Paradise.

I was taught that it was good to cover my bases.

When I was 25 my grandmother went in for a hip replacement.

She was 88 years old—adamant that if she did not get a new hip, she was going to be in a wheelchair by April. In January of 2016 she got a new hip and was bound to a wheelchair. She had a micro-fracture in her femur. This occurred sometime between going in for surgery, coming out of surgery, and her first week of physical therapy.

Three weeks later she was diagnosed with congestive heart failure.

She was filling up with water. Twenty pounds of water. At the time I wondered, Is this the same as drowning? Three weeks before she was not drowning.

My father told me doctors could control it.

The doctors said she did not have pneumonia.

I thought about whether it was possible to control drowning. Whether it was possible to control God. If this was all part of the Plan. I did not like God's Plan.

I am a blasphemer and this is my confession.

My grandmother needed a new hip not because of the wheelchair. She needed it because she was proud. It was hard to admit to herself, let alone her children, that she was dependent upon them for everything.

My mother and I thought she was crazy to demand something so risky. And my grandmother was demanding. She wanted her house on Grand Avenue, her 2000 white

Chevy Cavalier. She wanted to drive to camp, spend the night, go to the grocery store, drive to church.

My grandmother wanted to not be dying.

Lungs filled with fluid: not pneumonia. Body filled with water: not drowning. Congestive heart failure: not dying.

In the middle of winter in the Upper Peninsula, that is, March, the sun set before five o'clock. At the Holy Week services, the sun was always in the middle of setting, or below the horizon. The sky was vibrant red and orange when I went into the parish, and black when I left.

The sky was either on fire, or had burned itself out.

When my grandmother broke her rib twice over the summer in 2015, she spent weeks on Vicodin. Most of the summer, really. That's how she developed a tolerance for narcotics and when the body developed a tolerance to pain medication, those receptors became cruel. They fired and fired and fired again and created an illusion of pain. The brain turned against itself.

Does the thing exist if it is a malfunction of nerve receptors? Is this how Jesus felt in the wilderness when Lucifer showed Him the shining city?

Does God listen if I do not attend church regularly?

Do patron saints listen to prayers on behalf of other people?

Can angels and saints and God discriminate against love?

In January 2016, my father asked me, "What do you think? One month? Three? Nine?"

I didn't have an answer to give him. What was better? I didn't know what better meant in this context. Alive didn't seem to be enough. But wasn't it? It should have been enough.

I told him, "It would be nice if she could make it to July. So I could get back up to see her." In January, the whole family was looking at weeks, not years of life.

The last time I saw her, we were at camp, and it was spring, and Grandma brought her paper dolls with her to give to me.

When I was young, I played with them every day on the floor in Grandma and Grandpa's living room while Grandma watched the news and we waited for Grandpa, Dad, and my brother to come back from fishing for walleye.

Scarlett O'Hara was always my favorite. I paraded her around the living room in her beautiful green dress and Rhett Butler escorted her over the piano bench while sunlight refracted rainbows onto the carpet and the fan whirred in the direction of Grandma's feet.

I didn't open the envelopes at camp, but when I got back to my parents' house in Minnesota, I spread them out on the floor of my childhood bedroom, and put Scarlett back in her green dress.

The paper dolls made me feel close to my grandmother. They reminded me of the happiest moments with her. I wanted her to live until July so I could make another happy memory with her. One more short memory.

The Tenebrae service was the shortest. Our choir only sang one song during the service and it was nice to sit and zone out while the priest gave some homily about sacrifice. I had a hard time paying attention to the priest in general anyway. His voice was throaty and he said off-color things regularly about gay people, and single mothers, and people of color. I figured whatever his feelings were about sacrifice, they only really applied to a certain set of people. And as I was neither straight, nor Catholic, I was probably not included in this group.

It was enough to be in a church—the tradition of the thing.

Lit candles lined the aisles and the altar. It was warm and glowing and all of the peacoats and parkas and mittens hung in the vestibule. Everyone wore jeans and boots and sweaters that were vaguely clean. Tenebrae was the service where everyone came as they were. There was nothing to prove.

The altar was still dressed in purple.

My mother texted me, "Will you write a letter? Here's the address."

There was an art to writing a letter like nothing was wrong. Like she wasn't in an easy chair sleeping most of the day away. Like she wasn't consuming only 500 calories. Like she was actually able to complete most of her physical therapy.

I wrote her a letter in my "lovely" penmanship. Told her I was planning on making a trip to the Yoop that summer. That I was writing an essay about the S.S. *Edmund Fitzgerald.* That I was writing an essay about the logging camps her father worked at. Reminded her I remembered listening to his tapes at camp.

Camp was Grandma's happy place. Happier, even, than church. She sat in her blue recliner and put tapes on and her feet were always in white tennis shoes.

In the mornings she drank coffee in the glider on the porch and listened to the Escanaba River burble.

This was a type of ministry. A kind of holy.

On Maundy Thursday the service was longer. Still quiet, contemplative. Incense burned. Candles lit, and snuffed. There was no communion.

This felt a little like punishment.

I'm sure that was the point.

There was the before. And the after.

In the after, there are no more weekend trips to camp. Only the ones when her sons take her for the day.

A month after her surgery, on a Monday in February, I asked my dad how she was doing. He was heading back to Michigan the next week. He said he was okay with all of it. The fact that "all of it" implicitly meant "dying" didn't need to be explained. I wasn't sure I was willing to believe him. Maybe it was only that I was not okay with it. With her dying.

I had no home in the Catholic church, but I found other church homes up north. I stopped going to church when I was 23, after moving to North Carolina. In North Carolina, there was nothing there for me, and I remembered that the Upper Peninsula was coined as God's Country to the locals.

I was a long way from God's Country. In North Carolina, I was a long way from my grandmother.

Maybe I was not okay with her dying because she no longer felt like the grandmother who took me to the park, and the dollar store, and built dollhouses in her free time. Maybe I was not okay with her dying because I was not the child she took to the park and the dollar store anymore.

A couple weeks later, I got news that my grandmother's lungs were free of fluid.

But she was on oxygen. Oxygen is a fluid. Fluid pumped in and out of her lungs. It helped to put these things into perspective in this way. Somehow it made it easier to compartmentalize. I didn't know what "free of fluid" meant. I couldn't make sense of what it meant that I wanted her to be ill so there could be something to fix. A before. An after. A time to move toward where she ate three meals a day: full meals that we measured in platefuls instead of spoonfuls.

In my mind's eye I decorated her room like all the hospital rooms I'd seen, even though she wasn't in a hospital. She was in a nursing home. It didn't sound better. Nursing home sounded like an oxymoron. A lie. My grandmother hated being nursed. And she wasn't at home. She would never have dusty blue wallpaper, or salmon-colored throw pillows, or a bed with rails, or linoleum floors that never looked clean. And her room in the not-hospital would smell like urine despite the Clorox, despite the nurses. It didn't matter if it wasn't true. It's all I had to work with.

Five years before her hip replacement she made her sons promise not to let her die in a nursing home.

Good Friday was not good.

It was depressing.

It was the betrayal of Jesus. The Last Supper. The Upper Room. The men in the garden of Gethsemane. Pontius Pilate. The people in the streets, yelling, "Kill him!" The cross. The tomb.

As part of the choir, I had to yell, "Kill him!" And this was a betrayal of my own belief. I hated this part of the story.

At the end of the service, the lights in the sanctuary were dim. A single light illuminated the altar. The priest stripped it bare. Folded the purple fabric, took the candles away. Everyone was silent. We stared at the empty altar. The priest walked down the center aisle, swung the incense burner which clinked in the quiet. When he exited and the congregation was left with nothing but ourselves, we also filed out. It was just the rustle of people, and in my chair at the front of the congregation, watching it all happen, it must have sounded something like what happened all those centuries ago in Jerusalem.

I had the distinct feeling that God was not in church on Good Friday. It was only the people.

We want our parents to be our parents always.

There is no tutorial on how to be the parent of your parent.

My father called on a Friday. No news was always good news. He didn't start by telling me how his weekend went in Michigan visiting Grandma in the nursing home. He asked me about my week. About teaching. Classes. The usual. We ended the conversation with my grandmother. The gist was that she was stable: she could sort of walk on her own with a walker, as long as she had oxygen. Otherwise, she got tired. Her body couldn't hold onto the oxygen anymore. At least that was what it sounded like. When she went to the bathroom, she had to be off her oxygen; she must not have had a portable tank. When she got back, her oxygen levels dropped to about 70. "Fifty is dead," he clarified.

I asked about physical therapy, if she was still going. If she was strong enough to go.

"Yeah. She can walk about seven feet with the big chair, and six feet with the small one. Whatever that means." I didn't know what that meant either. But I guess that was progress.

"Paul is calling her confusion 'delirium,' not 'dementia.' The doctors aren't really sure what's causing it. They think when her oxygen levels dropped so low they may not have caught it in time, and that's what's causing her to forget." He told me she had moments of clarity. This was progress.

"Who knows how long she could last, now. Maybe months. She could still be around when you come visit this summer." He sounded so hopeful as his voice filtered through my phone. He sounded so different from a week before, when it sounded like we were past any hope of recovery.

I imagined my grandmother's new hip. Her new fracture. How a majority of patients with this type of fracture not only had a permanent limp, but the pain never went away. The way muscles and tendons fill out legs. How they atrophy if they are not used. The same way plants wilt without light or water. The way the brain skips over mundane details to get to the action of memories. I imagined my grandmother's leg swollen with water, painful to use.

At night my grandmother sometimes forgot she couldn't walk without assistance. She fell. She didn't hurt herself that time. But of course, her falling was how she broke her rib twice over the summer. How she developed a tolerance to narcotics.

The nursing home placed an alarm that went off when she tried to get out of her chair, or her bed on her own to alert the staff.

I learned that even though her lungs were free of fluid, she had pneumonia for two weeks. She aspirated on her food, and the particles settled into her lungs and that was how she got pneumonia.

"That's not the kind of thing that gets better." I tried not to sound frantic, but I'm sure it didn't work. I felt manic, wracking my brain for some answer I learned in some class at some point, but there wasn't one and I knew that in theory the doctors were doing what they could.

All my mother could tell me was "Well..." I could see her sitting in her chair, shrugging her shoulders, lifting the pitch of her voice. "Your grandma is still in the rehab unit in the nursing home."

She told me the physical therapists were giving my grandmother ten more days to prove to them that she could complete her therapy. If she couldn't, she'd move to the nursing home. The part of the nursing home that wasn't for physical therapy patients. The part of the nursing home that was for old people. My grandmother reminded us often that she was not old. Or she used to. I realized I couldn't remember the last time I heard Grandma argue that she wasn't old.

My mother did not sound hopeful in the way my father did. Mom and I think about things like aging in perhaps the same way. It's the introversion. My father looks out to the world while my mother and I look in to ourselves and try to find some traction, some answer there. Hope is harder to come by when we are so rooted in our own head.

But what was better? To be realistic in this case seemed to verge on the edge of pessimism, but optimism felt false. Fell flat. Like we were hoping for the best just for the sake of hoping for the best. And that seemed wrong.

Can people hope without setting expectations? Is it possible to hope for the best without believing it will happen, even just a little bit?

Saturday was Easter Vigil. It was the longest service of the week and because it was three hours long, and the eve of Easter, everyone showed up in their good clothes. Myself included.

I walked into the parish in a button-down shirt and slacks. I left the iridescent blue tie hanging on my doorknob back at my apartment and I felt self-conscious. The hope was that I would feel like I stood out less, but I didn't.

Despite singing in the choir for two years, when I walked up to the usher and smiled hello, she said, "Good evening, sir," while handing me a bulletin. I said thank you and watched her eyes get wide and her cheeks redden, but she didn't apologize and I didn't let her. The bulletin was a half-sheet of paper, front and back, and I stared at it instead of her and walked into the sanctuary.

When the lights in the sanctuary dimmed and went black, the congregation stood in unison to head to the fire outside for the lighting of the Easter Candle, and the lighting of all the little candles that every person was holding. I wasn't sure what the lighting ceremony represented. Maybe the light of the Lord, and how it would soon rekindle with His resurrection. It was hard to be certain though, because people kept shifting away from me.

We lit our candles in the narthex, away from the March winds. They were lit from the priest at the center, outward. The man in front of me turned around, a smile on his face, and a lit candle. I smiled back as I leaned my candle in towards his flame. He looked at me, up and down, up and down, up again. He saw through my button-down, and as he stared, his lips curved down in the way that ventriloquist dolls frown. I told myself his lips were just pursed, trying not to drip wax on the carpet, even though there was a wax guard. But he seemed very upset, and now my candle was lit, and I turned away from his stare to the boy standing behind me. I helped him light his candle, and when each flame flickered to life, we walked back into the sanctuary for the beginning of the vigil.

When it looked the worst, my father asked me to maybe say something at the funeral, maybe write something. I said yes because that was what I could give my dad, my dad's family.

But I had no idea what I wanted to say—what kind of story I wanted to construct for my grandma's funeral. I felt selfish for writing about the months after my grandmother's hip replacement, but I had no other way to cope. "Anticipatory grief," my dad called it.

"We're not trying to keep things from you. We just can't remember who we've told what." I was talking to my mother on the phone and I was upset, or frantic, or frustrated that I was under the impression that my grandmother did not have pneumonia when in fact she did.

I was aware that I could call my parents for updates, but I didn't.

I wasn't sure I wanted to hear the day-to-day.

It was more of the same, every day.

She needs oxygen. She's in pain. She's in pain. They can't find the right dosage. She should be on an antidepressant; the anxiety medication isn't doing enough. She just looks so out of it. She didn't recognize Marlene last week at all. She did not recognize her son yesterday. She's in pain. She can't breathe. She can't walk. She's in pain.

If you say a word enough times, it stops sounding like a word. If you write a word enough times, it stops looking like a word. Does it work the same way with sentences? Do the words stop holding meaning?

I was at the Easter Vigil service to sing the Litany of the Saints. They varied from year to year, in accordance with the baptisms and confirmations. This was my third year singing the litany, and this year I was away from the choir, having left the parish for a Lutheran church. But I came back to help out during Holy Week.

I sat in a pew by myself. The church was full of people but in my pew there was only one other couple, seated on the opposite side next to the center aisle. They would rather be smoked out with incense, and sprayed with holy water than sit next to me. There were going to be two hours of psalms and readings and hymns before it was time to sing the litany.

After I walked to the pulpit, and sang the names of saints, I walked out of the church because I was not welcome at the baptismal font, or the communion table, and I was not even welcome to hold a candle in the dark.

In the worst of my grandmother's healing, I was grasping at straws. Praying to saints who were not listening. Hoping that because the prayers were on behalf of a believer, that someone up there would take notice.

My grandmother is Catholic, so these things mattered to her. And because they mattered to her, I reasoned, they mattered to me, too.

I looked at patron saints for the elderly. But then I thought my grandmother would be offended I thought she needed a saint because she was old. There was a patron saint of arthritis. My grandmother had arthritis. It was what made her retire from her position as church organist.

There was a patron saint of chronic illness. This was, apparently, not the same as arthritis. But my grandmother also had emphysema, and congestive heart failure.

There was a patron saint for desperate situations. When I heard my father and his brothers talk about their mother, I thought maybe this was a desperate situation. It was all relative, and since there was a patron saint of epidemics, I didn't feel as bad calling on this one. My grandmother would probably be offended I was considering calling on St. Jude for her health. But it wasn't really for my grandmother. It was for Dad. For my uncles. So I wouldn't have to call on St. Rafka, or St. Colette yet for the loss of a parent.

Technically my grandmother was now handicapped, so there were four different saints to call on there, if I needed to. This felt like bargaining to me.

St. Rita of Cascia is the patron saint of impossible dreams.

I did not bother clicking on her link because I wasn't sure I wanted to know what that meant. There was the possibility, the probability, that St. Rita was not capable of granting any wishes. She would say that was God's job. Above her pay grade. Out of her hands. Her job was probably something like easing the anxiety that accompanied the realization of impossibilities. Of finding that dreams were exactly what they were: not solid. Not possible.

I made sure to ask my dad whether Father Fran was visiting Grandma in the nursing home. She couldn't go to church, hadn't been able to for a while now. I thought the priest visited every week or maybe twice a week to offer comfort to my grandmother, distribute communion. These are things that matter to her.

I imagined her sitting in her recliner, Father Fran pulling up a chair to sit next to her. Maybe they read a devotional together; he read the week's gospel and a psalm. He recited the words that turned wafers into flesh, grape juice into blood. He placed the bread on her tongue, poured a small amount of juice in a cup, blessed her, sat with her. The consistency was important.

She held her rosary in her hands. It was the rosary I brought back from Notre Dame when I went on a choir tour to Europe in high school. When my mother was taking care of her over the summer of 2015, Grandma told her it was very calming, and I found comfort in that. I liked that I could bring my grandmother comfort.

Maybe all I was looking for is comfort. A patron saint of my own. I wondered if people who were not Catholic were allowed to call on saints. There was a patron saint for earaches, lost items, tax collectors, alcoholics, philosophers, natural disasters, thieves, and wine, but there was no patron saint for queer people.

At the Easter Vigil service, the font was a pool, a wishing well of blessed water and cream-colored marble. During my second year singing Litany of the Saints at St. Mike's, I went to the baptismal font. I was greedy after over a year in the parish to feel closer to God, and so I followed behind the other choir members even though I was not supposed to. The men and women of the choir liked me enough that they forgave this transgression. As long as I did not take part in communion, they let me have that one moment to be a participating member of God's church.

Still, I felt like I had to justify this, and I remembered that I was baptized into the Catholic church, if not confirmed into it. A priest poured water over my head three times, and declared me God's child first, and my parents' second. This was what my grandmother wanted.

The water of the font was cool, and I touched my fingers to my forehead, chest, and each shoulder. *Remember the cross. Remember my baptism.*

When I moved to the South at 23, I found a church within the first month. Church felt like a source of stability in a new place, so I joined the choir because the people were nice. They were excited that I wanted to sing with them.

The choir director, a man in his eighties, was a retired university choral director, and was nearly blind and nearly deaf, but he loved music. His stubbornness reminded me of my grandmother. He greeted me after my first Sunday and by Wednesday I had a robe, a folder, and a seat in the rehearsal space.

They were good people, who tried very hard to sing. I was the youngest member of the choir by 30 years, though, and there were some things good intentions couldn't hide.

The choir was terrible. Half the members couldn't read music, or were tone deaf. Another 25 percent were so old that their voices wobbled and it was hard to tell whether they were singing the right pitch. Our director could barely see the music he was leading.

St. Cecilia could not save us, even if she wanted to. I thought she smiled anyway because we were trying with gusto.

I left my local church six months later after the preacher compared an atheist pastor to Satan tempting Jesus in the desert. It was the gatekeeping I hated. After the service was done, I hung up my robe, peeled my name tag off my folder and hanger, and walked to my car. I talked to no one.

My grandmother took a long time to leave the nursing home. But she did eventually go back to her house on Grand Avenue.

It seemed sometimes that all the pain was for nothing.

My grandmother went back to her house at the end of April. She visited camp when her sons came to the Upper Peninsula for trout fishing in May. She fired all the assistants who were hired to help her within the first week of her independence. We sat and hoped that she would not fall, or try to go down the stairs to grab whatever it was she thought she needed.

Her sons took her to camp. Her friends drove her to church. Meals on Wheels brought her dinners.

She was nasty in her old age. Angry at her license being taken away. Angry at her sons for making it so. I was angry at her for being angry.

My grandmother didn't die. We kept holding our breath every time there was a hiccup, but every time, she bs.sounced back. Maybe not energetically, but enough to keep the house on Grand Avenue.

I kept writing letters to my grandmother because I don't think prayers work all that well, and I don't believe people when they say they can feel people praying for them. My grandmother can hold my letters and I can hold hers. In our written words we are closer than we have been in years. In our written words I am learning how to have a relationship with my grandmother as an adult.

I think maybe writing letters is a religious experience, and so is reading those letters. It is filled with ritual, and proper language, and etiquette. I don't have a rosary and I don't have saints, so I keep all the letters we write and thumb through them like prayer.

Siren Song

Lake Superior on a calm day has a depth clarity of over 100 feet. In shallow waters, boulders appear to be just below the surface. Near shore, trash creates a timeline of occupation: plates, tires, bikes, phones. Old dock pilings dot the lakebed in even lines. And on days when her surface is glass-smooth, it's possible to see some of the 350 wrecked ships resting on the lake floor. They all look blue so far down.

I grew up with the lake. I've visited her, lived by her shores, returned to her year after year. I've seen the ships underwater. They're as real as anything. One has its toilet seat up. Everything sits in the same way as the day it sank. The lake's frigid water acts as a refrigerator—preserving the ships and the sailors who went down with them. The bed of Lake Superior is part museum, part graveyard.

I've never seen the S.S. *Edmund Fitzgerald*, but I've seen her bell. Recovered and back on land, it sits in a glass case, polished and shining. Every year it tolls 29 times.

The S.S. *Edmund Fitzgerald* leaves port from northwestern Wisconsin on November 9, 1975. Her belly is heavy, loaded down with 26,000 tons of taconite pellets. She is a giantess, one of the country's largest freshwater ships, the so-called Queen of the Lakes, though in truth, her long body is less than glamorous—a dull maroon the color of dried blood. A workhorse on the water. After 17 years, she breaks her own records, carries tremendous loads, and still, they push her forward.

The captain, Ernest McSorley, is on his last voyage before retiring, heading east once more across the vast expanse of Lake Superior toward the Sault Lock System, gateway to Lake Michigan. A quiet man with a mischievous streak, he's spent four decades with the Great Lakes. He has sailed across Superior November after November, taught many men how to work a ship, seen everything the lakes are capable of creating. He knows the *Fitz* is tired, but after 40 years on nine different vessels, he's got a certain steady confidence.

The crew of 29 men hears of a storm to the west, gathering energy over the Great Plains, rolling over Kansas, heading north. But from the safety of the harbor, McSorley looks out at the clear skies ahead and sees a quiet woman. Novembers are always bad, but maybe this storm will veer. Standing in the sweet cold breeze, he thinks—hopes—they'll make it through this trip without much protest from the lake.

It used to be that, in sailing, it was bad luck to name a ship after a man. The S.S. *Edmund Fitzgerald* is named after the president of Northwestern Mutual Life Insurance, who wanted to build the biggest freighter on the biggest lake. There was her ill-fated nickname: "*Titanic* of the Great Lakes." Maybe it is greed that cursed the ship. But there were omens from the start. At the christening, Elizabeth Fitzgerald had trouble with the champagne bottle. She swung and swung and the bottle would not break. Then the *Fitz* refused to launch. Men hammered away at the great logs holding her up. And when she finally did slide into the water, she immediately crashed into a pier, sending up a great splash while a crowd of thousands looked on in horror.

Everyone knows how the *Titanic* sank, ripping itself open on an iceberg and splitting in two. But the sinking of the S.S. *Edmund Fitzgerald* is one mostly of speculation. The accepted report states she slowly filled up with water as the hatches leaked, and, when the storm hit, it brought too much pressure to her already burdened body. She's said to have sunk like a boat in a bathtub.

But I don't think that's how it happened.

I think the lake sank the ship.

In late fall, the lake's surface water is still relatively warm. So when Arctic air from Canada descends, it collides with the warmer air hovering over the lake, and massive low-pressure systems build. For a time, the winds scream and whip the lake into a jagged frenzy, creating rogue waves. A rogue wave is any wave that is twice the size of surrounding waves. Rogue waves rise out of large bodies of water when the currents and winds push several waves together to become one. These monster waves exert a breaking force seven times greater than what a laker vessel can sustain. They are large enough to register as objects on radar and impossible to outrun. While we have a general understanding of how they form, we don't yet have the tools with which to predict them. They resist understanding, nearly impossible to study because they appear seemingly out of nowhere. Where rogue waves shouldn't occur, they do. They are usually singular, unless they're in a group of three, what we call Three Sisters.

And the wind that whips up these terrible waves? Sailors call it the Witch of November.

We name women who spend too much time with nature *witch*. Dub her dangerous. Unpredictable. Call her *other*. The land is something to fear, or exploit. To be a witch is to love the natural world more than the things human hands have made. And so we burn her. Or we revere her. We tell stories about her to frighten children of the woods or the water. Though some of us may ask her for help. Or maybe just mercy.

In Greek and Roman mythology, when the Titan Kronos unseated his sky father, Ouranos, the god's blood rained down onto his wife Gaea, Mother Earth. And from that spilled blood rose the Erinys, the three Furies. Tisiphone, Alecto, Megaera: Avenger of Murder, Unceasing Anger, Jealousy. These three sisters hear complaints, pass judgement, dole punishment. To incur their wrath is to be relentlessly hounded.

Another trio, the Moirai, the three Fates, together hold a person's life. Clotho spins the thread of destiny. Lachesis holds it out. And at the moment of death, Atropos cuts the thread. The Fates and Furies are goddesses, but the line between *goddess* and *witch* is thin.

When it comes to bodies of water, we often use contradictory terms. In one breath, they are women, naked and angry: a jealous lover. In another, they are cleansing: a baptism. A goddess. A witch. We name things we want to control after women.

But a name can be a kind of offering, too, a protective spell. For we also give vessels the feminine pronoun: a ship is a buoyant body that cradles sailors as they cross lakes and oceans and rivers. A type of mother: she carries her children safely through another woman's unruly body. Or at least that is what she was made to do.

When I learned the word *genderqueer* at 20, I learned a new way of understanding my body. I tried out the label *trans* but it didn't stick. It felt too much like I was picking an identity that forced me into a box, restricted me in a new way. Genderqueer felt broad, expansive, fluid. It felt encompassing. Encompassing like my lake. I could let the lake and the language hold me in ways I did not hold myself—that is, gently.

When people talk about questioning their gender identity, they often use words like *grappling*, *coming to grips with*. There's a holding and slipping and missing and reaching and reaching and reaching. The turmoil I felt, and continue to feel, about my body, my gender, is more like Lake Superior in November than a calm day in July. But when I float in the lake, I am a body in a body and she is soft, even when I am not.

I spent my most formative years with this lake. I swam in her waters as a child, diving for rocks. I hiked along her shores and built castles in her sand. Later, in college, I let her waves lull me to sleep as the northern lights shimmered over a dying fire. I used to think I knew everything I needed to know about her body. I was superstitious in my adoration of her. *If I love her enough, she will stay the same forever.* But lakes are bodies. And bodies do not—cannot—stay the same.

At 20, I did not want new pronouns to accompany my new-found identity. A singular "they" pronoun didn't yet exist in the queer community's vocabulary. There were complicated options that tripped on my tongue, caught in the back of my throat. And besides, there was something powerful in keeping my feminine pronouns, my feminine name, in forcing strangers to reconcile a dissonance that I felt all the time.

I don't want to name Lake Superior's body "it." "It" as a pronoun takes away agency. Takes away a life. There is too much power in the water. Too much I can't name.

On the morning of the tenth, the gale warnings are upgraded to a storm warning, and the temperature drops. The winds are high, gusting at 50 knots. The waves rise to 18 feet. Lake Superior's blue water turns gray. Without sunlight, the clouds meet seas at the horizon line, and the division between water and sky blurs. The *Edmund Fitzgerald* tandems another ship, the *Arthur M. Anderson*. The two ships keep tabs on each other, on radar and radio, stay close along a northerly route heading east for the safety of Whitefish Bay. The harbor there is one of the only docks between the port and the Sault Locks big enough to shelter such giants.

It starts snowing hard in the afternoon, and the *Fitzgerald* is 17 miles ahead of the *Anderson*, visible only on radar. A wave crashes over the deck and breaks one of the fences. The water drags the screeching, twisted metal into the mouth of her, swallows it. Superior presses against the belly of the ship, pushes her sideways. McSorley radios *Anderson* Captain Bernie Cooper: "I have a fence rail down, two vents lost or damaged, and a list. I'm checking down. Will you stay by me till I get to Whitefish?" The *Fitz* slows down, lets the *Anderson* gain on her again. There is a sense of safety in proximity.

In the Upper Peninsula, when storms roll in, the lake often feels warmer than the air. When my brother Peter and I went body surfing as children, I huddled in her water against the chill of the wind, waded out to just above my knees—*No farther!* Mom called—as another wave rose up behind us. Dad waved beneath a gray sweatshirt, *Psychology Today* or *Newsweek* in his lap, a pile of towels folded next to him.

It's easy, now, to forget about all the times I caught the wave wrong and Superior tumbled me over and over on the hard sand bottom. Turned me around until I wasn't sure which way was up. Everything turned monochrome. The gray of the water and sky, in my memory even the sand looks gray. And maybe there, in all that gray, were the Fates, holding a thread as thin as the wind. Maybe I became part of the lake for a moment. Maybe the Fates considered me as the lake turned me over—watched as I reached my hands out, instinctively searching for the bottom, stretching my legs for sand to stand on. When I finally found it, I pushed up toward the gray sky, stood in the surf coughing the water from my mouth, my nose, my lungs. I shivered, thankful the water wasn't deeper, then huddled back down, squatting there in my pink suit, my blue suit, my tie-dye suit—year after year after year. In Superior, I was always sure of my identity: I was part of her. Breath caught, I waded back out to the waves. Together, my brother and I glided toward the beach, walked up the sand to wrap ourselves in warm towels.

By 5:30 that evening, gusts rise to 70 knots, and waves peak at 25 feet. They swat at, then destroy, the life boats of both ships.

At 7:10, the *Anderson* checks in with the *Fitz.* The pumps are going, doing their best to clear the water flooding the decks and the hold. Captain McSorley says, "We're holding our own."

Seven minutes later the *Anderson* loses the *Edmund Fitzgerald* on radar. The *Anderson* reaches Whitefish Point before 8:00, but the *Fitzgerald*, the larger ship that was ten miles ahead just an hour ago, is not there. The Queen of the Lakes never arrives.

That evening may have gone something like this:

A witch cackles in the sky. The lake below is a bubbling cauldron, waiting for a nasty spell. Beneath the rough water she finds copper, iron, and basalt. The copper was laid down ages ago when glacial ice dredged the land, and the iron formed long before that, when the Earth was still new. Cooled basalt rises up, ready for rebirth. Above it all, the witch snatches snowflakes, fierce winds, the night itself. Blood meets water, her recipe complete. A transformation brews.

She trains her eye on this grand rusty Queen, jealous of her size and extravagance. The witch sees the endless hunger of men. How they have hollowed out the land, searching deeper and deeper for more ore, more copper, more nickel. How they have weighed down their Queen with this quarry, worn her out. But no man looks at the lake and thinks she could be any more than she is. The witch knows better. The lake, the sky, these are endless, and the ship is temporary. Peering down between clouds, she releases her spell.

Three Sisters gather their strength. Three Furies, three Fates, charge toward the freighter. They are walls of water, taller than any of the other waves. Their whitecaps trail terrible veils from their crests. The first, the smallest, rushes over the hull, empty of sailors, fills the ship with water. The second sister follows close behind before the water can drain, heaves herself over the railings, smears her 40-foot body across the length of the *Fitzgerald*, weighs her down, and waits.

The third sister, the tallest, throws her body on top of her sisters. Their combined weight presses the bow of the ship low. Then all that ore down in her belly, all 26,000 tons of it, cracks the hull of the *Edmund Fitzgerald*, and the waves keep shoving her down. And it's too much.

After reaching the harbor and not seeing the *Fitzgerald*, Captain Cooper asks the Coast Guard if they were looking. Their responses sound like excuses: *Their boats weren't big enough to navigate the seas. They were searching for another small vessel that didn't make it.* The *Fitzgerald* wasn't a priority. She's so big, the Coast Guard thinks maybe she ran aground or got off track. They assume she'll be in to port soon. They say the *Anderson* should go searching.

Cooper knows what it means when a vessel doesn't reach the harbor. He does not want his ship to join the *Fitz*. But he goes back out anyway, hoping to see something, someone. He finds nothing but gasoline tanks and empty life preservers.

Two days later, a crumpled lifeboat will wash up on shore, its metal frame bent and battered, a hole punched through its bow.

What were those final minutes like? Certainly the men would have known the options were grim for a sinking ship in the middle of a lake in the middle of a storm. Did they hope beyond hope that the *Anderson* crew would catch them, drag the body of the *Fitz* to bay, and climb through the half-submerged frame to find them all clinging to pillars?

Maybe as the winds scream, the men cry. Or pray. Maybe one thinks of the single crease in his wife's forehead; another of ice skating with a child on these same frozen waters. Maybe they think of slow cups of coffee on a Sunday morning, the quiet crinkle of a newspaper, the comfort of sharing space with their love.

Everything happened so quickly. Captain Cooper thinks the men didn't even know they were sinking until the very end. He thinks the *Fitzgerald* started slowly sinking in Wisconsin. A tear somewhere in her body, bogging her down as she chugged across the lake. Even so, she still might have made it had there not been a storm.

When the third sister arrives, perhaps they think it is a just another big wave, and they will pop up in a second. But they don't pop back up.

Maybe the men sit on their bunks and listen to the lake pounding against the ship, the steady whir of rushing water like radio static. Maybe they hear a cackle in that howling wind. And then, the deepest moan as the body cracks in half.

And then, water.

And the sisters fill up the bodies.

They all are one now, the bodies and the sisters and the lake. She is made whole by the storm, a whole that is made and remade again and again. In this one body there is no need for names. Everything is quiet and blue, and in the dark, still.

Ode to Your Body

On my beige futon in the middle of winter you told me you were genderqueer. I had only just graduated from college, but I was sticking around and working as a nanny while I waited to hear back from graduate programs. I was 22 and you were 21 and it was nice to have someone in my life who could understand how I saw my body. How other people saw my body.

On my beige futon at the beginning of spring two months later, you told me you wanted to start hormone replacement therapy.

You talked about top surgery and facial hair and probably packers. You told me you weren't genderqueer anymore. I feel selfish now when I think about how hurt I felt at the time.

This is an ode to your body. To the soft of your sternum and the fuzz on your arms. Your sharp jawline. The straight line of clavicle. To your short hair. Your unshaven legs. To your wide shoulders, strong from rugby. To the tan lines on your biceps from helping your mother herd chickens and goats, and gardening on the weekends.

And this is an ode to your body. To your still clean-shaven face. To your breasts you do not let me see. To your stomach: the curve below your belly button where biology would have said a baby should grow. To hips your mother lent you and you have been spending most of your adult life trying to give back. I love them. I love their points, like wings. I drew circles right below those bones, traced all those smooth curves along your torso. I loved that they were the pink of skin that remains untouched by sun.

This is an ode to a body that is not your body now, but was your body then. This is to your body then and your body now, and the way you grow and shift and change and the indistinguishable moment your body became new. Became a body not recognized by your mother. How do you convince your mother you are the same as you always were, just with different words?

Maybe that moment came when I saw you again eight months later. Or maybe that was the moment I realized that moment had already passed. That you were another you who was like that person on the couch that winter night. That the you I knew and recognized hadn't really been you. And the you in front of me was close. But separate. Farther away.

You were a person to get to know again. To re-meet.

Maybe I was not me anymore either. We had to reintroduce ourselves. Not strangers. We knew too much about each other to be that.

I was the one who left, and you were the one who stayed. I insisted that we break up at the end of the summer when I moved to North Carolina for graduate school. I didn't want to try the long-distance thing when so much of our lives were in flux. Three years of school for me and 18 months for you, and I couldn't fathom what we'd do in the interim.

A thousand miles and eight months of school made us new people.

The moment happened at a bagel shop in Marquette on the first sunny day of my visit in May. I sat at a metal table outside and waited for you to walk up the hill from your rusted-out black truck. I picked at the bagel on my plate; I had arrived early and didn't want to eat without you. I was always early.

Next to me, a little girl climbed on the bike-shaped bike rack, perched herself on the seat, hooked her bare feet around the body of the rack, yelled to her mom as she stuck her wobbling arms out to either side of her beanpole body.

You tapped my shoulder, and I turned around, smiling in surprise that you were behind me.

"Grab a cup of coffee," I told you, holding your shoulders. It was so good to see you. I watched you walk into the cafe, wait in line for your small black coffee, and I sat to sip on mine.

You should have seen me before I got on the plane to leave North Carolina ten days before our coffee date. I hadn't heard your voice since before you started testosterone the previous October. I was too afraid to miss something that wasn't really mine to miss. I was too afraid I wouldn't recognize your voice over the phone.

I heard too many people tell me couples didn't make it through transitions. Too many things changed. It wasn't just vocal cords. It wasn't just the broadening of shoulders and slimming of hips. It was puberty all over again at twenty-two. That ravenous hunger. Pendulum mood swings. *You fight or fuck*, I heard from other people with trans partners.

Maybe I didn't try to take our relationship to North Carolina because I was too afraid to be your support system from a thousand miles away. Maybe I was too afraid of the way your body would change. I loved your body for the way it inhabited a space that was all your own. I loved your body because it was yours. Because it was not a cis-man's body. I was too afraid I would not love your body on testosterone. I was too afraid I would not recognize it in the same way I wouldn't recognize your voice.

I don't think I can tell you these things.

I think it probably makes me a bad person. At the very least, a bad friend, a worse lover. Because your body has always been a man's body. I don't know how to navigate this space. The language does not allow for these nuances. Language changes everything.

Before you came to understand you were a man, you were genderqueer. We had that in common.

We are always everything at once.

Years have passed since that trip in May. You are now a you that you were not while we sat in the coffee shop and I marveled at your gravelly voice, your sharpening jawline, your peach fuzz. You were so proud of your peach fuzz.

I was happy that you were happy.

People use the word *bloom* all the time when they describe someone coming into their own. And I know that you would probably bristle at a so blatantly feminine adjective, but it fits. That day on Third Street, for the first time you were proud of your body. It was finally starting to feel like yours. This is an ode to a body that is always yours.

The Geography of Pronouns

In June of 2016, the summer before my third year of graduate school, I drive 767 miles from Wilmington, North Carolina to Northampton, Massachusetts to visit my friend J—. I leave at 4:45 in the morning and at 7:35 PM I arrive in front of their house.

Before I drive up, in a phone conversation J— asks me which pronouns I want them to use when they introduce me to people. I ask for a couple days to think about it.

Up until now, with the exception of a semester in undergrad, I have always gone by the name and pronouns given to me by my parents. Going by anything else feels too difficult. If I am unwilling to change my name—a decidedly feminine name to which I am, perhaps stupidly, attached—it seems unlikely that anyone is going to hear my name and ask about pronouns. My name literally means "lady." When I introduce myself to people, more often than not they tell me things like, "I have a great aunt named Martha!" As a kid, this was mortifying to me—to be compared to someone's older relative. My great aunts loved crocheted doilies and refused to serve orange juice after breakfast. They put their hair in curlers and wore costume jewelry. Their houses always smelled of perfume, soaked into the shag carpeting and couches. In my eyes, they were the ladies.

Even though now I sort of enjoy making people think about their great aunt Martha, it sounds exhausting to be constantly responsible for correcting people's assumptions. Thinking about it—the sheer number of times each day I would be required to educate people—makes my stomach turn. It feels heavy on my chest. I leave it at that and content myself with feminine pronouns.

Hate isn't always something you can see.

Sometimes it is a rip current, yanking people out to sea. The inability, or the refusal, to recognize gender as a spectrum feels kind of like that.

Sometimes hate is the constant accommodating queer people give to self-proclaimed allies. Hate is the amount of time queer people dedicate to educating cis-het people without losing patience. It's that cis-het people require queer people to speak candidly about their experiences. Hate says, "Prove your queerness." Queer people consent to this because to do otherwise would dis-endear us to straight people and perpetuate stereotypes of the "angry gay" as if we do not deserve our anger.

What we do not tell our allies is, "We owe you nothing."

When I get back to J—, I say, "Could you use they/them please?"

I phrase it as a question because I still can't shake the feeling that this request is an imposition. I can't convince myself that I deserve this.

At my request, J— replied, "Of course!"

J— has, for some time, been referred to as my gender friend. About six months after they came out as genderqueer, I followed at the age of 20 during our sophomore year of college, finding that the word felt good, felt right. Since then, saying gender friend became an easier way to define our identities. There is nothing complicated about either "gender" or "friend" at the surface level, and so for a brief moment we become uncomplicated. Uncomplicated only in the way that we do not have to explain ourselves.

Language is just another way to physicalize gender. Another way to own our bodies and our identities.

After gliding under the radar, it is easy to forget what validation feels like. It feels like floating. And, like floating, there is the awareness that it is happening, but nothing has really changed. The act of validation doesn't change anything. It just takes away some of the weight.

J— and their girlfriend E— take me to a bar a few blocks from their house. My impression is that J— knows everyone in town. Working at a coffee shop has its advantages. They greet the bouncer at the door who smiles and takes our IDs from us.

"Enjoy," she says.

We head to the back and sit down at a high top. The light above us casts a hazy orange glow, just bright enough to read the menu.

When I hear my pronoun for the first time, I think I blush, and my eyes grow wide, and I am grateful for the dim lighting and the alcohol. I don't say anything, but I want to say thank you or could I hear that again.

It is the ease with which validation is possible that surprises me. Outside queer communities, pronouns feel large and cumbersome. Something to battle for. The secret is that they are not. We've just been convinced everyone else's comfort should come before our own. Be as small as possible. My gender is an inconvenience. *You take up too much space. You're already queer. All you do is write about being queer. Couldn't you write about something else?*

Hate makes me choose between self-affirmation and safety.

In Northampton it feels like I don't have to make that choice.

When I visit, it is one week after the mass shooting at the Pulse nightclub in Orlando, Florida. Memorials and rainbow flags line storefronts in Northampton. In Wilmington I don't see a single pride flag. Instead, I see Confederate flags. And "Make America Great Again" bumper stickers. These are portraits of a country. I am part of a portrait divided.

Hate requires grief to be private. Hate says, "Get over it. Pull yourself together. It could have been worse."

There is the sense that Northampton grieved collectively. I don't know what that feels like. It has been too many years since I've felt part of a community. I only know how to grieve privately. Even in Wilmington with my friend who is from Orlando, I feel like I cannot impose on her grief. She talks to her friends from high school, begins crocheting—her stitches so tight I wonder how she manages to stick the hook in. When we talk about the shooting, I float above the conversation. Only one friend checks in on me. But also, what is there to say? I've been told by straight people that the queer community has made "so much progress" and I stare at the headlines on my phone and I think marriage equality is not enough. It is so clearly not enough.

In Northampton, I am uncomfortable looking at the memorials. Melted candles line the sidewalks. Ribbons and streamers and balloons and posters hang off fences. Writing fills the windows of shops and houses. Rainbows are everywhere. I don't know how to access the support available at the moment when J— points out a chalk heart on the sidewalk, says, "I drew that." They smile wide—a part of a community come together at this time. I feel nothing. To be queer and numb feels better than to be queer and feeling too much. J— has the support to feel too much. They have the ability to be worried about the safety of all their friends. I am stuck pushing the anxiety back and back and back.

It is hard to not be bitter.

Northampton gives me the opportunity to feel too much. It is exhausting to cry, to feel so far from a community, to know I'll go back to MAGA hats. Wilmington is not what I hoped. But I try to take comfort in the reminder that places like this exist. Places where my gender is not inconvenient. Places where strangers don't stare at me, or if they do, it isn't obvious. There are places where mothers in coffee shops refer to me as a person instead of a lady, or woman.

I remember Wilmington is not permanent.

When people in my graduate program ask if I am staying, they are surprised when I tell them no. And I am surprised that they are surprised. Then I remember that for many people, this beach living is paradise. And paradise trumps so many other things.

They say it's their job to stick around to change the policies.

"Be the change," they say.

"I'm tired," I reply. I don't have the stomach to challenge the system. I am too afraid. And I am unashamed to be afraid.

"We're fighting the good fight," they say. And they all say this. They want me to join in—stand on the street corner holding signs, start up a rally, hold a pride parade, start a petition, sign a petition, call my representatives. "There's power in numbers," they say.

"I know," I tell them.

"That's good," I tell them. It is good, but I don't really care if they are fighting the good fight, or just making it through the day. More often than not, I am only making it through the day. When I see more Confederate flags than

American ones flying outside houses, I am only making it through the day. And this is a kind of fight. But sometimes it takes a reminder that existing is a political act, and in those moments, I wish that existing could not be a political act. Sometimes I need to be told that my fight does not, and should not, look the same as every other person's fight.

When I leave Northampton, and return to North Carolina, I tell myself I will leave my gender-neutral pronoun in the north. I come back to ma'am, and lady, and woman. It would happen regardless of what I wanted. It will continue to happen.

Gender isn't on cis-het peoples' radar. It doesn't have to be. Pronouns are taken for granted, lumped in with pants that fit, and shirts that fall the way they're supposed to, and bathrooms that don't require IDs to enter.

When I moved to North Carolina I was told that "ma'am," and "miss" were signs of respect. The implication, of course, is, "Don't be upset about this."

"Don't make a fuss."

"Don't talk about it."

The implication is, "Just be glad no one is harassing you."

I am not glad.

I tell my students to call me by my name and nothing else. And even though I say this, on every one of my students' assignments "Ms." comes before my last name at least once. I smile when they "ma'am" me, a small ache right below my throat.

When I told J— what pronouns I wanted them to use, I didn't tell anyone else for months. I was terrified all my friends, even the queer ones, would look at me and laugh.

When I asked J— to refer to me using they and them, in the back of my mind I thought over and over that I would not be able to keep these pronouns. I thought I couldn't.

A few months after my visit to Massachusetts, I go to the counseling center on my school's campus to get counseled for a whole bunch of stuff, but mostly to talk through my gender. In small places—safe places—I begin using gender neutral pronouns: in a queer group on campus; with my friend from Orlando. In my therapist's office, I go by "they." During one particularly difficult session, after having talked through a rough class when I got "lady'd" more often than usual, my therapist tried to comfort me by saying, "Martha, you are such a wonderful woman, who has so much to offer her classmates." She didn't even realize she was doing exactly what my classmates did.

Not enough people use singular-they pronouns in Wilmington for it to be in the common vernacular of either my graduate program or the community at large. "They" as a pronoun is still novel here. It sticks in the back of people's throats in the same way that ze and hir caught on my tongue when I first came out as genderqueer.

I feel very small when I am in Wilmington. And the smallness makes me say, "I'm not an activist." I'm not here to change the world. In high school, that's what I thought I wanted, but that's not what I want now.

Maybe someday I'll want that again.

While living in Wilmington, people ask me again and again why I am uncomfortable. I stare at them, disbelieving. They must have blinders.

On my campus, the 2016 election digs trenches among the students. Campus Republicans scrawl "Build that wall" in chalk all along the sidewalks and we haven't had a rainstorm in weeks it seems. The letters are haphazard, white and blue and green. It is clear art was not the goal. "Make America great again" is painted on signs and boulders in garish white and red dripping text.

On my campus a professor targets a queer, Muslim, woman of color on social media, and when students complain, he says *oversensitive*; says *PC culture is ruining freedom of speech.* When students complain, the chancellor tells the campus community that nothing that was said was "threatening."

It sounds more like, "Just be glad it isn't you."

I'm tired.

My queer siblings feel unsafe. My queer siblings are being harassed. My queer siblings are getting killed. And we all have action plans and emergency contacts listed in our phones and our wallets, and we have those for when we attend parades that are supposed to be a celebration of love.

Hate tells us, "Don't get shot."

Hate tells us, "It could be worse."

Hate tells us, "It's your job to fix it."

Hate tells us, "You're not in danger."

I want to tell hate that there is a student in my classroom who bought their first binder. I want to say that I am the only teacher they have who asks what pronouns they use. And in another class, I have a student whose parents put her in ex-gay therapy, and she wrote her story and let me read it. This matters. I want to tell hate that, in these moments, I am not tired. In these moments, I remember why pronouns matter. Why stories matter. And it is in these moments, I want to tell hate I'm not going anywhere.

I'll Like You for Always

When I am 22 and freshly graduated from college, I begin taking care of two babies. The job comes by accident. The babies' parents work full time as teachers and the nanny quits suddenly. I love kids; I need something to do. I start at the end of January when Michigan snow drifts around the doors and trees. Everything is white and gray and brown in January. But the babies are bright.

We start our days with dance parties. The toddler, Addy, loves music and will dance to almost anything. John Allison Weiss plays from my computer, which Addy calls her 'puter. Ollie is secured to my chest in a Moby wrap. I remember to take my sweatshirt off first this time. The first week, I started sweating just putting the thing on. Now, I am getting better at it, leaving just enough room for Ollie and me without either one of us getting fussy about being squished. He drools all over it and I remind myself that this is normal.

Addy grabs my hands and jumps, thumping out of rhythm with the music. "Spin me!" she cries, and I explain how I can't with Ollie, so she runs around me giggling instead, occasionally pausing to catch her breath. She exaggerates the action by bending over and placing her hands on her knees. She huffs and puffs and then jumps up, rejuvenated as if by magic.

The album has been on repeat for the past three days, and I contemplate the implications of letting a toddler listen to a song that starts with, "There's wine on my shoes from the time that I spilled it." Such things are probably not considered "best practice," but she likes the sound of the synth piano and acoustic guitar that pings its way through the hallways that she now races through in her stocking-feet. I stop her to take off her socks so she doesn't slide on the wood floors and crash into the exposed brick. But I would not have thought to do that if her mother hadn't told me first.

Sunlight reflects off snowdrifts in the front yard. I consider closing the blinds, but it has been over a week since the sun has shown. Winter in the Upper Peninsula is gray most days. Blue and green dots my vision as I blink the sun's reflection out of my eyes, and I wonder what this must look like to anyone passing by on the street: my hair sheared close to scalp, a nondescript t-shirt, baggy jeans. A baby hugs close to my chest, teethes against my finger and the sage green fabric of the wrap.

I spend a lot of time worrying about what this picture must look like. I don't consider myself to have the "mothering" look, despite the fact that I would regularly define myself as such among my friends.

Our walks start with the black and gray stroller. Used tissues sit under an empty sippy-cup; a collection of rocks, pinecones, grass, dirt, and leaves pile up in the opposite cup-holder. These are treasures that cannot be thrown away. Two sweatshirts are shoved into the bottom mesh compartment alongside one of Ollie's shoes that I haven't thought to bring into the house yet. He took it off one walk, and wouldn't keep it on, so I shoved it into the basket.

I buckle him into the front seat, the straps awkward around his bulky sweatshirt. I remembered all the times mothers and ladies at church cooed at babies about not getting cold. I make sure the straps aren't too tight; call Addy over from her pile of pine needles. She brings me some as a gift. They go into the cup-holder with the other loot. I think about how nice the colors are: the dried yellow dandelion, the copper-orange pine needles, the taupe of dried weeds.

I like long walks: it creates a schedule that doesn't include a television prior to lunchtime. It is early May, and the sun finally heats the Earth to a comfortable temperature. The winter was long, and the sight of buds on trees and the smell of dirt underfoot is enough to make me giggle as my shoes tap softly against the asphalt path that follows the lake where icebergs still dot the shoreline. Grass is greening beside me, and Addy points, "Marfa! Flowers!" and I stop the stroller so she can go pick the only green weeds available. Everything is a flower. Last weekend she yelled, "It's summertime!" while running in dizzying circles. It was 70 degrees.

She pulls the weed up entirely by the root and hands it to me so she can pick a more dazzling array of other weeds. Most of them are still dry and dead. She does not mind, and neither do I.

After about twenty more minutes intermittently walking and stopping and collecting and dropping, I ask, "Ready, Buggaboo?" She turns, pulls her fingers from the soil, nods, clamors into the back of the stroller, appropriately named *Sit n Stand.*

"Are you going to sit or stand?"

"Mmmm...stand." She always chooses to stand. She climbs in, holds on to the handles built for her. I remind her she must always hold on, otherwise it isn't safe.

With her permission, I turn the stroller around and head toward home. "One, two, three, zip-zap."

Nearing the halfway point, she leans on the one measly black strap at the back of the stroller. Restless. We are passing houses on a back road because the sidewalk that follows the highway makes me nervous, and it's too loud anyway.

"Addy, if you can't stand, you need to sit on your tuchus." A woman walks up to collect her mail. She is in her early sixties, wears a light gray crewneck sweatshirt. Her hair is graying, and she smiles at the bundle of children in front of me.

Addy reaches up her small hand, waves slowly, and says hi. The woman says hi. She stops. We stop.

"What's your name?" She hunches down, waits for a reply, to which she gets a shy silence. I volunteer a name for the woman, and another for the baby boy sitting in the front of the stroller peeking around behind his chair.

She asks me how old they are and I tell her, "Addy just turned two, and Ollie's nine months."

She turns back to Addy, "Are you a good helper for Mommy?"

As the little one nods, I sneak in a, "Do you help Momma cook dinner when she gets home from work?" and it dawns on the woman that I am not these babies' mother. A look somewhere between embarrassment and apology crosses her face. She clarifies, "Oh, you're the sitter, then?" And I laugh. Tell her I get the children during the best part of the day.

I wave to the woman, and she waves to Addy, and Addy waves to the woman, and Ollie smiles and giggles. I try not to think of them as "my" babies, but my toddler points straight ahead and says, "One, two, three, zip-zap." She does not see me smiling behind her, pushing her forward in the direction towards home.

I am trying to understand how to name what it feels like to be a caregiver. It feels like being a parent, but not. I feel like I am somewhere between sitter and parent. If it is possible to be in between those two things. Or maybe all full-time babysitters become this attached, call the children they care for theirs because it is easier than naming the parents first.

Still, I wonder how I am mistaken for "mother." Because, at 22, I still think of *mother* as feminine, and I am not. But maybe there are things that name me "parent." Maybe it is just the fact of the stroller. Of the children. The sippy cups and tissues. The collection of pine needles and rocks and dried leaves I haven't had the heart to throw out.

Being a full-time babysitter includes a lot of crying. And sometimes it is not the babies who are crying.

In March I am hearing back from graduate programs. It is mostly bad news. Three rejections so far. I get most of the news while I am sitting at the table at lunchtime. Addy is trying out lettuce right now, and her plate is a collection of spring mix greens—no dressing—, and clementine slices, and toast with cream cheese because I let her choose what she'd like to eat. Today it is toast with cream cheese.

The day has been an easy one: Ollie is in his high chair; Addy is in her booster seat. They are eating quietly. I check my email.

Some MFA program has sent me a form letter about "Thanks for applying" and "We regret to inform you" and "cannot offer you admission at this time." At this point I have stopped really reading the name of the school.

Everyone has told me to not be discouraged. Lots of people don't get in their first year of applying. This is not really comforting. I feel unprepared for the world outside of college and thinking about waiting another year to apply again makes my stomach drop.

I go into the bathroom.

"Marfa? Where are you?"

"Marfa's just going to the bathroom, Bug. Be right out."

"Ohtay."

I spend a minute crying in the quiet of the green bathroom. I breathe in the scent of laundry detergent and dryer sheets. Swipe at my eyes. One more breath. Smile wide, come out, say, "How's lunch, Buggaboo?"

"Good."

"Good. I'm glad."

It is one-thirty in the afternoon. I have only just managed to put Ollie down for his nap. From Addy's room I hear, "Marfa, Marfa, Marfa," and I hope she will soothe herself back to sleep. I clench my hands against frustration. She hasn't napped all week, instead knocking on her closed door, and giggling when I go to tuck her in again. And again. And again.

This has been a week of crying during naptime because I am so exhausted from a teething, sick infant, and a toddler who is outgrowing her naps. I do not like to admit that I need the forty-five minutes to myself, but I do. I need forty-five minutes to eat lunch and sit on the rocking chair with the two cats, Oscar and Lucy. To hear nothing except cats purring—one on the arm rest, the other on my arm—and listen to the muffled sound of Ollie's stuffy nose through the door. I hold my breath as I wait to see if Addy calls again.

It does not go quiet, and Addy's cries get louder until her door clicks open and a little face pokes out from the darkness. "Marfa, I poop-ded." And of course, she has. She had an upset stomach all morning. I couldn't even convince her to eat string cheese.

I turn on the light and hoist her onto the changing table, notice that the diarrhea has seeped out of her diaper into the white cotton t-shirt she is wearing, and she starts crying.

The shirt is lifted off, thrown onto her soiled bed sheets. I hush her softly, tell her, "It's okay, Bug. We'll get you all cleaned up, okay?" and she nods looking up at me, bare-bellied, sniffling on the plastic-coated pad. I pull new clothes from her drawers, a new diaper from the basket.

Clean, clothed, and dry-eyed, I lift her off the table and tell her to go to the living room while I strip her bed. The toddler-bed sheets fold into a small bundle. I spray disinfectant on the changing table and the bed and everything smells a little fresher and less sickly, but I still wish for warmer weather to crack the window open.

I toss the bed sheets into the washer and walk into the living room. Addy tucks herself into the deep cushions on the couch, legs stretched out so they almost reach the edge. She stares out the window, her sniffling turning to snuffling, softening as she calms. There's no way she'll be getting back to sleep now, so I say, "Should we just cuddle for a little bit?"

Nodding, she says, "Can we wrap up?"

"We sure can, Bug."

I drag the over-sized throw from the opposite side of the couch and drape it over her lap, my lap. She grabs fistfuls of fleece and hoists it toward her chin.

"Do you want to watch Elmo?"

She nods her head. I put my arm around her, and she nestles into my chest. I wonder if it's evolution that allows children to fit just right or if parents just know how to make space. If children know how to fold into grown-ups just so.

I turn on the TV and Sesame Street welcomes us back for another visit. I close my eyes for a little bit, listening to Addy's quiet breathing.

After visiting my parent's house, I bring back my childhood tub of crayons. The container is true blue and has a dinosaur riding a skateboard on it. When my brother and I were very little, this was Peter's. Mine was purple. It later held the markers. The markers have long-since dried out, but crayons never seem to go bad.

There are so many crayons, it is hard to clip the clasps shut. I bring sheets of paper over to the table, strap Ollie into his booster seat and give him some teething toys to play with and Puffs to eat. Addy bounces into her chair, kneels. She doesn't like being strapped into the booster seat, and for things like crafts, I don't push it.

"Let's start with just a few colors, and then we can switch them out. Sound good?"

"Mmhmm, yep." She has paper and crayons; she'll agree to basically anything.

"Let's pick out five." I slide the tub over to her, and she picks out a ballpoint pen, a sky-blue colored pencil, a purple crayon, a brown crayon, and a red crayon.

She loves the feel of the pen in her hand: the thin, exact line that scrawls across the page, how it makes sharp points all over the paper.

Ollie is gnawing on his giraffe teething toy, and it squeaks with each gummy bite. It's his favorite, and I like it because it looks less like a puppy toy.

"Now what color should we use?"

Picking up the blue pencil, she says, "Mm, I don't know."

"That's a great choice." I point to the pencil and lean on my palm, trying to watch Addy and Ollie, who has finished eating his pile of Puffs and consequently thrown all his toys off the table. It is getting harder and harder to find things to entertain him. I give him a crayon, hoping he doesn't try to eat it, and tell myself it wouldn't be the worst because they are nontoxic.

He puts it in his mouth. I take it out. He throws the crayon. I do not give him another one. I put his giraffe back on the table. He throws it. Addy asks for another crayon. I give her the drooly one. She says, "Ew" and puts the crayon down and holds her fingers up for me to clean. I go, "swish swish" with my palms and say, "All better!" Magic. Hand her the red crayon. No, not that one. The purple one.

I take Ollie out of his chair. He crawls over to Addy, pulls up on her chair, reaches up toward her paper. She pushes him down. I tell her not to do that as Ollie pulls up on her chair again, and this time, she just points at him and says, "No, stop it, Ollie."

Ollie crawls to me and holds my fingers and pulls himself up and we are content for a full five minutes.

At naptime, she climbs into bed as I turn on her lamp. I pull up floral sheet, reindeer fleece, pink baby blanket, and purple plaid comforter.

"What should we read today, Bug?" She leans over the bed and picks up the blue book with a boy wrapped up in toilet paper and I almost tell her no, how about a different one, but she insists *Love You Forever* is the book of the hour.

The room turns the pages a terrible tint of Pepto-Bismol pink as the sun filters through the magenta curtains. I manage to get through about half of the book before a cork lodges in my throat.

She says, "Keep reading, Marfa."

"Just a sec, bug." Deep breath. Fill lungs. Exhale. Sniffle. I am not too proud. "I'll love you forever. I'll like you for always. As long as I'm living, my baby you'll be."

She tries to ask me to read another, but I roll her over onto her tummy, tell her it's time to close her eyes and go to sleep. The light clicks off as I pull the chain.

"Love you, Addy. Sleep well."

"Good night."

My mom never read *Love You Forever* to me or my brother because it made her cry. It never made me cry as a child and I'm not sure how to talk about the reasons why the book makes me cry now because my babies are not really my babies.

It should not be possible to grow so attached to children who will not remember me. They are too young. Brain development and all that. I am a blur, literally, for Ollie. Object permanence, or something. For Addy, I am five months of Play-Doh; cheeseburgers made from fake doughnuts and plastic bananas; choosing the green pants with pink sweater, or yellow shirt with striped pants; barrettes, or ponytail; John Allison Weiss or *Frozen* soundtrack. Time goes too fast when age is measured in months.

By May, Addy has taken to labeling everything she sees. It has become a game on our walks to point out and label as many objects as we can find together. We are practicing using words to understand the world. Addy stands in the stroller, waves her arms maestro-like while her brother flails in his t-shirt.

"What's that, Addy?"

"Mm, a car."

"That's right. And what color is the car?"

"Mm, purple." Every car is purple.

"No. What color is that car?"

"Mm, I don't know, blue?" Unless it's blue.

"No, that car is red!"

"Yeah! Red!" And she claps her hands. I have a brief moment of panic that maybe she is colorblind and maybe I should tell her mother and then I tell myself to stop overreacting.

She points to a fenced-in yard and asks, "Does a gog live at that house?" Her mouth hasn't figured out how to make the conflicting consonant sounds yet.

"You know what, I bet there is. What do dogs say?"

"Arf! Arf!" She pauses, says, "Is it a boy gog, or a girl gog?"

"I don't know. We would have to meet the dog first, right?"

"Right." She loves meeting dogs. It's one of her favorite activities after meeting cats or people or picking dandelions. On this particular route there are dogs, cats, people, and dandelions. We go on this route a lot.

"Is Ollie a boy or a girl?" I ask.

"A boy."

"Is Addy a boy or a girl?"

She giggles at this switch. "Addy is a girl."

"What about Momma?"

"Momma's a girl."

"Daddy?"

"Daddy's a boy."

"And what is Marfa, Addy?"

She turns her head and looks at me. "Mm," she says, "you are—Marfa boy."

It surprises me to be named something that feels right. Or maybe it feels right to be recognized as outside the lines by a toddler. It makes me hope it is possible to understand without really understanding. To know parenthood without being a parent. To hold mother outside the lines of femininity. I don't know if that is more beneficial to me or the rest of the world, but the thought is there, and I hold it close.

Addy trips and falls and when she stands up, she is crying.

"You okay, Bug?"

"No—" and she points to her mouth.

"Did you bite your lip?" and she shakes her head. "Did you bite your tongue?"

"Yeah, I did."

"I'm sorry, Buggaboo. Are you going to be okay?"

"Yeah." She turns around to go play again, but comes back to me. "Will you kiss it and make it better?"

I consider saying no, but her tongue is already stuck out, just like any other booboo. "Sure, Bug," and I give her pink tongue a light peck and she giggles and runs back to her Play Dough.

It is my last day in Michigan before I pack a truck to head to North Carolina. I am at a church luncheon with Mom and the babies. I try not to think about how I'll miss Ollie's first birthday, and his first steps. How I'll miss Addy's first dance recital. How important they are to me.

Mom and Addy and Ollie are just about ready to go: the diaper bag has been re-packed and filled with more snacks than diapers. Mom and the babies hover at the door. I give hugs and kisses to Ollie, and Mom hunches and whispers something into Addy's ear. She giggles and runs at me and I lift her up in another hug.

"I want a kiss right here," and I point to my cheek.

She perches on my hip; little toddler arms wrap around my neck. It is a peck more than a smooch, but she holds tight.

Empty the Land

If the land is our mother, then the lumber barons of the late 19th and early 20th centuries took a rusty scalpel and performed a double mastectomy and left her body to stitch itself back together. It wasn't until the mid-20th century that anybody thought it might be a good idea to at least try reconstructive surgery.

The land will never be the same.

My queer body is not the land.

But if I choose to have top surgery, if I choose to remove my breasts, instead of binding them down with Lycra, then that would be the only difference between me and the barons: choice.

My queer body is not the land, but the way people have flattened it is not so different. The result is the same: an empty space.

My queer body is read by others as "woman."

I don't know what it means that we name the land "woman" and when we beat her and gut her and spill chemicals into her, the only phrase we come to after is *They raped the land*. I don't know which came first: violence on women's bodies, or violence on the land. But in the end, the violence is labelled with the same language.

I don't know why we call things that can't speak "she."

My great-grandfather was a lumberjack. He was also a husband. He also loved horses. And he loved woodcarving. And he loved his only daughter.

But my great-grandfather was a lumberjack and when I, at 25, listen to the tape recording for his town's celebration of the bicentennial, he sounds as though he is longing for a time that doesn't exist anymore. Nostalgia for a land that doesn't exist anymore, can never exist anymore; he helped make it that way.

I can know that longing for work that he loved is not the same as longing for flattening trees. It is not equivalent. But I could write the essay where I twist those lines into equivalency. I could write the essay where my great-grandfather is nothing more than violence-hungry. I never met him—all I have of him are these tapes, the stories my family has passed down to me, and the land I think he loved enough to work in every day. All I have is the wood-carved model camp he created to remember a piece of his life, a piece of history.

We can't know the future. We can't go backwards. But we can remember.

When I was a child, maybe five or six because it must have been before t-ball, my dad taught me the right way to throw a ball. He taught me to make an "L" with my arm and "think *up* on the ball." When we threw the football, in order to really make the lesson stick, he challenged me to throw the ball over the pine tree in our backyard.

The tree was nondescript as far as pine trees went. It had long, soft needles, that, as a child, I ran my fingers through like hair. I think Dad told me it was something like Douglas Fir, but maybe it was a different tree. The tree in our backyard had needles that always looked brighter and lighter than "regular" pine trees. This tree was special because this tree taught me how to throw a football.

When the lessons took place, in the mid-nineties, next to our vegetable garden and impatiens, the tree looked huge to me. Like 10 feet tall. When Dad stood on the other side, it would have been easier for me to throw the ball under the tree rather than over it. But Dad was an enthusiastic coach and as soon as I managed to hurl the ball over the pine, that would be the end of catch. A reward of some kind, reaching the goal of getting the ball to arc over and into Dad's hands was an accomplishment worth ending on.

Ten years after our initial lessons took place, in 2006, a hailstorm ripped through Northfield, and the pine tree in the backyard lost a few of its branches. The more mature trees in our yard survived pretty much unscathed, but the Football Tree ended up looking a little lopsided as it guarded Mom's roses. For my whole childhood the tree grew in a straight line upwards with its branches in a tidy teardrop shape starting about five feet from the ground; now it had a bald spot on its right side. We all worried the tree wouldn't survive the shock of losing a quarter of its branches, and that winter after the storm it looked like it really wouldn't. Needles turned brown, and the tree looked, if possible, emaciated in the snow.

But then spring came, and summer came, and the one-year anniversary of the storm arrived, and our roof was fixed, and our gutters were fixed, and the Football Tree in the backyard was still green. Still growing.

There is a story in my family about a white pine that grew near the Sturgeon River camp of my dad's childhood. In the 1970's, my dad's family took trips during the summer to, initially, a camper in the woods, and, later, a small cabin that may have really resembled a shack more than a cabin, but it was theirs, and my grandpa built it himself.

It wasn't a beautiful camp, but it was near the river, and the property butted up against the Chippewa State Forest: protected land with big trees. Grandma and my uncle Paul took walks during the day while Grandpa and the other boys went off on fishing or hunting adventures. The only other option was staying in the hot camper.

Together Grandma and Uncle Paul found an old white pine. A tree that had, maybe miraculously, survived the lumber barons of the early 20th century. It was over 80 feet tall in 1976, and today measures probably over 100 feet. My grandma could not wrap her arms around the trunk that day in the woods.

The tree became a beacon of some sort for my grandma. Something to come back to during those long summer days when the sun rose before six, and night didn't fall until well after ten. In my family the tree became legend.

The Sturgeon River camp was sold in the late 1980's. By 2000, Uncle Rich began the process of building the Lundin family a new camp.

When Grandpa died in the summer of 2003, Uncle Paul went out to the old Sturgeon River property. The outbuildings were all still there, although they hadn't been used since the mid-eighties. The roof on the cabin was overgrown with moss, and the outside was rotting away.

But in the back of the property, on the edge of the state forest, Grandma's tree was still there. Strong and tall. I imagine the crown of the tree stretching upwards and around in a wide arc starting 75 feet up. The bottom of its trunk wide and the bark coarse against my uncle's fingertips.

In the Iroquois Nation's tradition, the white pine is called the Tree of Peace. They used its bark for medicines.

Grandma's tree must have provided some steadiness for my uncle. Even though the camp of his childhood could hardly be called a camp anymore and even though Grandpa was gone, the white pine was still strong and growing.

In elementary school, my brother Peter and I went to our daycare after school to wait for our parents to pick us up. During the summers we spent all day there, running around outside with the other kids. The school age kids didn't nap, so while the little ones were asleep all the older kids went outside to play under the pine trees. Peter practiced his climbing. He was a fearless boy, and growing up he was all lanky limbs and long legs. Watching him, it looked as if he threw his arms and legs over tree branches and clamored up and up and up until he was at the top of the tree.

He was told not to go so high, but it didn't matter. Peter was the oldest of the school-agers. And every day during the summer he climbed his favorite tree and when he reached the top he shook the branch with his feet, jumping up and down, trusting the elasticity of the branch, and the anchor of the trunk.

I was not a climber. Sometimes I held on to the lowest branch, reachable by tiptoe, and climbed my feet up the trunk and hooked them around the branch and hung upside down, but I never learned how to get upright. It looked like it required letting go, and I was too afraid of falling.

In high school, my brother was voted by his tennis team to be "Most Likely to Become a Lumberjack."

He liked flannels and he was tall and he did all the things people think lumberjacks would have liked: the woods, hunting, fishing, and singing beer songs.

To my queer body, flannel feels like camouflage.

Camouflage comes from the old French slang, *camouflet*: a puff of smoke. There and then not. Flannel hides the curve of a bust through an illusion.

In high school, I don't wear flannel. I am afraid to ask my mother to buy me anything from the men's department and so I don't ask for a flannel shirt. I buy a single pair of men's jeans when I am 17 that disappears the curves of my body.

I don't start wearing flannel until I am 19 and in my first semester of college. On a trip to Wal-Mart, I head towards the men's department and pick up a gray and navy checked flannel button down. It doesn't fit me properly; it's too big. But it is warm and soft and I feel better when I wear it.

When my uncle Richard began building his camp in 2000, the property was almost entirely cedar swamp.

Cedar is a soft wood, good for kindling, easy to split once it has been cut down. Cedar thrives in soggy environments, places where the water tables rise to meet their wandering roots.

Uncle Rich had to clear the land; a swamp was no place to build a cabin. Preparations had to be made, and in this case, those preparations meant chopping thousands of feet of lumber. The cedar and hemlock and jack pine could all be used for firewood, and so, once those were cut and collected, they were stacked to season for a year and dry out.

But the stumps of those trees were sometimes large, unwieldy. They fit in a fire pit, but were rarely good for firewood. They took too long to burn, took up too much space. Stumps and leafy, spindly branches were collected and pushed together using a backhoe. The sound of the engine drowned out the cracking and snapping of the branches as they broke over one another. In the building of camp, there were many piles of branches.

The piles got burned one by one by whoever visited the camp. One by one, the bright green of soft and flat cedar needles burned an acrid, dark gray color.

Stumps and branches and logs that haven't dried out hiss and snap against the heat of the flames. When wood has not had enough time to dry out, they are called greenwood. Greenwood smokes before it burns.

There was no illusion here either. The wood did not puff at all. The smoke lingered in the air; it poured from the center of the stump, through the fingertips of the branches. The trees did not want to disappear.

But the needs of the property had to be met.

Uncle Rich sent photos of the construction site to us in an envelope. I remember the colors red, gray, and brown. I don't remember the green flashes of healthy cedar leaves. It's possible they had dried out to the ugly orange of dead pine needles.

We visited the camp for the first time the following spring when I was ten, and all I could see was brown and gray. The cabin looked like a shiny new penny, freshly sealed. The water hand-pump out front was fire-engine red, and there was forest green trim on the outbuildings.

In trying to piece together that first trip, I come back to the image of puddles. So many puddles. It was a wet spring; it must have been. All I can remember is the mud: iron-stained soil making copper-colored puddles around a copper-colored cabin. The grass hadn't been planted yet and so the only color besides the brown and gray of a wet summer was the man-made parts of camp.

The building of the camp felt like a justifiable destruction as I walked along the porch.

My queer body can be acted on as if it were inactive. As if my body were somehow detached from my consciousness. As if the two were somehow not affected by one another. It is possible that people see my queer body the way I, at 10 years old, saw the trees that were chopped down at camp: a thing that could be gotten rid of.

I can manipulate my queer body any way I choose. It is possible that for some time when I was 20, I saw parts of my body as temporary. I wanted top surgery, so I bound my breasts flat and relished the feeling of my ribcage expanding against the restriction of the binder. I researched testosterone injections and saw the way queer bodies changed over time: how jaws squared, brows became thicker, shoulders widened, and the distribution of fat to hips decreased. I reasoned that if I started taking testosterone when I was 21, then by the time I was 23 my body would feel more mine. Would be read by others as not-woman.

But by the time I turned 21 I had abandoned the binary almost entirely and passing was no longer first on my gender priority list.

During the lumber boom, there was no illusion. There was no camouflage. There were only trees to be cut down, and money to be collected. Despite the fact that in the early 20th century, the Upper Peninsula's industry was made up almost entirely of lumber camps and mines, most of the public didn't know anything about the life those men led. Sorcery happened in the forests. Men went into forests and left a landscape that had been gutted from the inside out.

The lumber barons of Chicago and Ohio gutted the state of Michigan. And it didn't happen in a year. It didn't happen in ten years. But by 1925, the huge white pines, and cedar, and oak trees that had made the Upper Peninsula so desirable in the first place to the men in the big cities had been almost levelled.

In 2011 there were finally more trees than there were in 1920. But fewer than one percent of the forests is considered old growth, or virgin, forests.

When Grandpa E was in the woods, most of the 300-year-old, eight-foot diameter trees of the late 19th century had already been cut down in the Lower Peninsula, but there were still tracts of forests in the Upper Peninsula where old growth stood.

I do not know what a 300-year-old tree looks like. It feels unfathomable. In a photo of a winter logging load, two horses pull a sleigh with 50 logs. The men seem small, perched on top of the logs, but the base of the trees look to be only about four feet across, and I still don't know how it's possible that a tree could exist whose base is twice the size of the lumber in the photograph.

Boogerman is the tallest Eastern White Pine in the United States. He is 186 feet tall after a storm blew his

21-foot crown off. He has a four-and-a-half-foot girth and lives in the Great Smoky Mountains.

"Boog" is one of the last trees that look like what my great-grandfather saw.

The trees that my great-grandfather was responsible for cutting and skidding and loading were old even before men in Philadelphia signed a declaration. Grandpa E was part of a legacy responsible for the erasure of a landscape, and I am trying to figure out what that means exactly: how a state that completely relied on lumber and mineral deposits could strip a landscape, and leave. The lumber barons flattened her; the miners hollowed her out.

In 30 years, the barons were responsible for stripping 19.5 million acres, and left the land unplanted. Moved west, the same way they stripped West Virginia and moved to Michigan.

Michigan still relies on forestry as one of its major industries. In modern forestry, trees are cut down in waves. Instead of cutting everything and leaving nothing, lumbermen cut some, replant, and when the rest of the forest has been systematically harvested, the saplings that were first planted will be ready to be chopped again. By leaving some, there is the illusion that the forest is not disappearing.

In 2003, when I was 12 years old, I started riding the bus to school again for the first time since kindergarten. The middle school was too far away to walk, and so, at 7:05, my brother and I walked down to the end of our cul-de-sac and waited across the street under some pine trees for the bus to arrive at 7:15. There were six trees hiding the apartment complex just behind them. They were stocky pines, with long needles that looked fluffy. The trees never seemed to get taller. But maybe the trees and I were just growing at the same rate, and so the perspective was always the same.

One died every few years and they were never replanted and it seemed to take forever for the stump to be removed and for grass to be seeded.

Thirteen years later, when I turned the corner to my street to visit my parents, I counted the number of trees left: three.

The trees mark a passing of time. I'm waiting for the last one to die. I wonder what it will mark in my life.

When I listened to my great-grandfather's tapes at 25, it was the second time I was hearing them, but maybe the first time I really understood what was happening. The first time I listened to them, I was 15 and I was sitting with my grandmother, his daughter, at our camp. His voice was tinny on the tapes as they crackled and whispered in the background of his interview. The tape player was sitting next to Grandma on a table beside her dusty gray recliner. It was hard to hear what he was saying from across the cabin, so I just listened to the lilt of his voice.

She had a copy of the tape at camp, and a copy at home. I liked to imagine that she listened to them a lot, now that they were the only place left she could hear her dad.

When I listened to the tapes at 25, I heard her in Grandpa E's voice. A phone rang in the background of the interview, and it sounded like the red rotary phone in Grandma's basement.

Our camp is not like his camp. We have electricity and running water. The closest thing we have to what Grandpa E would have had are a couple lanterns that my grandmother bought at St. Vincent DePaul Catholic Charities. She lights them at night. We don't even have to rely on burning wood during the chilly autumn because we can turn on the radiator. When Grandma is at camp with us, we usually use both the radiator and the fireplace. The sleeping loft gets hot, but we just open the window upstairs before going to bed.

I never knew my great-grandfather. He died before my dad was even married, let alone had children. But we are a family that passes down stories, and we are a family that is most purely ourselves when we are in the Upper Peninsula of Michigan. It seems right then that the Escanaba historical society, in 1976, would interview Grandpa E. A celebration of the bicentennial. A celebration of the history of the Upper Peninsula.

Maybe what I am listening for now is a sign that I am Grandpa E's great-grandchild. I am trying to find what the legacy is. I am trying to find out if the legacy is in the trees that he helped cut down.

Between 2010 and 2014, I try to spend as much time as I can at camp. I am at college in Marquette, Michigan, just a 40-minute drive from the cabin. In the fall, I meet my dad and Uncle Rich there for their annual hunting trip, and as I turn off 480 onto the camp road, I breathe a sigh of relief.

The road is iron-stained sandy soil. Uncle Rich doesn't own the first stretch of road, so it gets progressively rutted and pot-holed as the years stretch on. But I have driven it so often, I know the zigzag way through the forest to avoid the worst of the holes, and the worst of the rocks.

I drive like my dad toward camp, anxious to arrive and head into the woods. My car goes too fast along the track, and my pulse speeds up searching for the big landmarks: the stretch of road that opens up alongside the power lines;

how there used to be trees that acted as a scrim but those got carted out a few years back, and how now it's just a prairie of tall grasses. I slow down along the field so I can look for deer that sometimes stand in the knee-high dried grass and stare at my passing car.

After the power lines, there's a stretch of road that is lined by poplars on both sides. In 2001, when the camp was brand new, the poplars were the first trees to sprout next to the newly bulldozed road. But they grow quickly: first one foot, then three, soon five feet tall and quaking in the wind with their wrist-sized trunks and their spindly branches. In 2013 they are taller than me, and tall enough that they arch over the road, nearly meeting in the middle. It's a magical scene, especially in the spring when the leaves are just popping, and they seem to glow as the sunlight streams through like a stained-glass window.

Then there's the stand of birches right before the locked gate. The birch bark stands stark in white columns. If I am lucky, I get to see them before their yellow leaves drop to the ground. Scenery in the Upper Peninsula turns brown after the leaves fall as everything waits for the first snowfall.

The last stretch of road before I reach the cabin is lined with tamarack pines. They are pine trees that lose their needles every autumn. The needles turn yellow—the same yellow as the birches—and then drop to the ground one by one. Tamaracks are one of my mother's favorite trees, and as the years go on, more and more sprout until the last image before the cabin is a curtain of golden needles in the fall.

After finishing my first year of graduate school in North Carolina in May 2015, I come back to Michigan to visit camp. I reach the stretch of road on the way to the property line where the dirt is copper-orange, and poplar trees line either side of the track and arch over, nearly touching treetops. Their leaves should have been bright green: the kind of green that only happens at the very beginning of spring.

But today, there is no tunnel of poplars.

Ten feet on both sides of the road has been flattened. The saplings lie in heaps, waiting for a truck and men to take them away.

Driving past them, the clear sky visible above me, I know that all it took was a chainsaw and a day to do the clearing.

I can know that clearing is necessary. Trees that grow too close to the road can fall, and though they are skinny—barely as big around as my arm—they are heavy, and cumbersome to move. By clearing the edges of the road, it makes it safer for vehicles. I can know that the absence of the poplars will allow dogwoods to grow, and grouse to nest.

I can know it to be a good thing, but still, I can't swallow the lump in my throat at the way the landscape changed. The trees pile up and I want the pickup truck to come now, to clear them away so that they do not rot and go to waste. I want to watch them haul the trees away; I would watch them burn the piles if they weren't so close to the forest that the trees used to be connected to. I want the poplars to be used so that they are not just useless brush piles—trees that are nothing more than a liability to the people who own cabins and use this road to get to them.

But I won't get to see the truck load the piles up, and I won't get to see them burn down to a pile of ash. I'm heading to my family's cabin that is still the color of a new penny.

It is easy to think the legacy Grandpa E passed down is one of erasure.

My queer body is a thing that can be erased.

When my uncle bought the property that now holds our camp, he cleared most of the trees. The birch, poplar, cedar, tamarack, and jack pines were cut down, chopped, and their stumps hauled from the ground. My uncle filled in the swampy parts first with gravel and then sand and then soil, and then he planted grass. Camp is not so much a cabin in the wilderness as it is a rustic resort. It means nothing that we are a 30-minute drive from the Tall Pines convenience store on the outskirts of Gwinn, Michigan. The cabin and the property on which it sits is manicured. Tailored.

There is a pump from the river that can be hooked up to a sprinkler so that the grass is always lush and green. Camp is our family's favorite place to gather and circle around the fire pit in our cushioned lawn chairs while we listen to crackle of fire and the burble of river.

It is our slice of paradise in the middle of the woods: a man-made meadow and cozy cabin and quiet river away from our jobs and cities and obligations.

Our camp is not a lumber camp. We go to leave work behind. But in the fall, when I follow behind my father in a borrowed blaze-orange jacket, and look at the frost framing the leaves on the floor, and marvel at the sky¬—how everything looks brighter in the cold—I can't help but think Grandpa E must have thought so too. Must have been awed at the snow drifts in winter. At the sharp smell of sap in autumn. These are things we must share.

Erasure is too simple. My queer body is a body that can be flattened, glossed over, removed from a common vocabulary, but I am not flattening, glossing, or removing my body from this place. Maybe what camp holds is the memories of things passed down. Is the ability to recognize how some things change, and how others don't. Maybe what I share with my great-grandfather is the knowledge that there are things that should not be lost. There are bodies that need remembering.

The Bound Body

In the winter of 2014, Lake Superior freezes in great sheets of ice and snow, and when the satellite shows images of the lake, it shows a black-veined blanket of white and cracked shorelines.

Before the lake freezes over, a small storm whips up. Waves crash against the break wall, spraying water over the barrier, into the air, freezing a little bit each time. The next day the wall is covered in ice inches thick, the far side spiked with horizontal icicles. Marquette installed a gate on the break wall a few years prior to keep people off the wall during storms, and it too is bound in ice.

November is no time to play chicken with the lake. The lake always wins.

The winter the lake freezes, I stop binding my breasts.

I don't know why that is.

The thing is, the lake never completely freezes. It's not actually possible for the entire body to freeze completely over. There is too much water. The record keepers started to write down how much of the Great Lakes Basin froze over in 1973. In an average winter, the basin is 30 percent covered in ice sheets that blow across the lakes with the wind. Over 90 percent is considered completely frozen. Lake Superior freezes in 1979, 1994, and 2014.

From Duluth, Minnesota to Sault St. Marie, Michigan, there are 31,700 square miles of water that makes its own weather. Weather that closes the bridge in Mackinac and hurls boulders the size of trucks onto the road in Marquette. It floods the streets of Duluth.

So that winter in 2014 when the lake is 94 percent ice, the wind howls through Marquette and the snow comes from the north in Canada and the west where the land was flattened out under the weight of the last glaciers to recede 10,000 years ago. That winter the wind blows and the lake freezes and the north side of Presque Isle looks out over a landscape of icebergs ramming into themselves, replaying the way the lake began.

I haven't figured out yet how people become themselves. It is because I am still becoming myself. Lake Superior and her basin had one-and-a-half billion years to get to where she is, and she is still becoming.

A list of things I know:

That winter, I am a nanny to two children under the age of two. When May comes and the little girl has her second birthday, we spend every morning going for walks with the stroller. I am asked if I am the kids' mother.

I am not in school anymore and I am waiting to hear back from MFA programs.

I feel nothing at all, or too much at once.

The lake is frozen.

I live by myself.

When the ice begins melting, I start seeing a person who binds his breasts. He has a very complicated relationship with his body and I know exactly how.

I categorize my life, perhaps, into spaces. Into places.

The winter the lake freezes, it does not unfreeze. The cold comes so early, and so fast, and so calm that when the ice forms, the lake has no choice but to lie quiet beneath it. There are no big storms that winter, nothing to break the sheets up. When spring comes, it comes slowly; the air over the frozen water has nothing to soak up, or soak into. April comes and the shipping lanes finally open while the lake remains 75 percent ice. May comes and the lake trout and salmon do not start their yearly spawning run because the water is too cold still. They stay hidden in the shallow creeks near the mouth of the lake. June comes and the air warms up and the beaches open and the townies bring their blankets and their rubber boots and wade out to the icebergs and spread their towels out and show their white bellies to the sun. It is the second week of June when the last of the ice recedes back to the lake.

There may be some level of logistics involved in my decision to stop binding. Unconscious, mostly. Children are very squiggly, and binders are not good for chasing and hopping. Most physicians advise against anything more rigorous than a walk, and after the first week of bending and chasing after a toddler, and Moby-wrapping an infant to my chest, my back hurts. My back hurts the way it hurts after binding for too many hours: a dull ache. The dull ache does not go away for five months because for five months I do not stop chasing and hopping and holding dance parties and tea parties and potty training and soothing two children. I wake up at six every morning to get to my babies by seven and I come home at four in the afternoon. I keep my blinds drawn, curtains closed. My living room glows in yellow lamplight and I only listen to Bastille and John Allison Weiss. On the weekends I can barely get out of sweatpants.

I can't fathom pulling bunched fabric down over my chest. It hurts to think about it. It hurts to think about gender, and so I don't.

This is a thing I do not tell other gender-benders.

I do not want my community to reject me. To tell me I am not that thing. That I am not one of them.

I hold this idea that maybe I am less genderqueer if I do not want to bind my chest all the time. If I struggle with this particular brand of presentation. I can't always tell if this is because I have always lived in places where it is not safe to be visibly queer.

The winter the lake freezes I spend a lot of time in the apartment of a woman who writes poetry. She reads drafts to me while we drink wine on her couch and, occasionally, we sit on the linoleum of her kitchen floor and drink margaritas while her Pomeranian tck-tck-tck-tck-tcks across the apartment with his stuffed bear toy.

She becomes stability. Her apartment is cozy with firelight and wood floors that creak.

At some point during that winter, I stop keeping track of all the details. Everything around me is a sheet of white, even Lake Superior. When I drive to work in the morning, I see nothing but a horizon-less landscape. So, when she says, "Give me your hand," I am caught off guard by the directness of her request. When I hold up my hand, palm facing hers, she measures the length of her fingers against mine and hers are longer, slender. She smiles when she tells me this, and I notice how there's a peak in her upper lip, and she reminds me to keep looking at the world.

The winter the lake freezes I do not visit Presque Isle very often. When I do visit, I trek to the back of the island and stand on Sunset Point and let the wind cold my cheeks until they are red and the sky is the blue of colored pencils, and the ice on the water stretches out and out in rough hills, as if the lake is frozen mid-wave.

The woman with the Pomeranian writes a poem called "Mohawk" and the speaker binds her breasts with Ace bandage wrap. I hear the drafts. The poem is right—in all those unexplainable ways that poems seem to get things right.

I know that Ace bandage wraps are bad. I never had to bind using them. But a few of my friends did before they bought a Nylon binder off the Internet, or a used one from an acquaintance.

After performing in a drag show and walking back to her apartment through the snow, a friend shows me the marks on her ribcage after unwrapping. Sickly purple and green and mustard-colored bruises stain her sides like prison bars. Accounts exist of cracked ribs because Ace bandages work like a snake: able to expand with intake of breath, but with each exhale tightens and expands less and less as the layers overlap. Until the diaphragm has to press against bone with so much pressure something has to give.

I can't explain to people why gender-benders gravitate toward bandages. It has something to do with the endorphins that run the first time we pull on a t-shirt and our chest looks more like how we always imagined it should. Endorphins transfer over to the sound of cracking spine, and bruised chest, and the thumping of pulse on sternum. The pain becomes some sort of beacon: it says, "I am here. I am trying."

Lake Superior was formed under the pressure from the weight of glacial ice a half-mile thick grinding over the landscape northward, and the basin filled with gallons upon gallons of water.

The lake knows something about trying to move forward.

It has something to do with the symbol of bandages.

Sometimes my body dysphoria feels like a tearing at my sternum. Like I am two halves and my bones are trying to right themselves while my skin holds it all together, unwilling to separate. My hands want to claw and press and push all at once. I cannot catch my breath, lungs filling and emptying again and again while my bones ache.

Telling myself it's all in my head doesn't help.

When I bind, I count my heartbeat as it vibrates against the back of my ribcage. I like how it feels like the Nylon is stitching me together.

I want to be stitched together. Bandages are reliable like that. They allow the illusion of a whole, patching holes in bodies, real and imagined.

When the toddler pinches her finger in a toy, she requires two things: a kiss and a *Dora* Band-Aid. It doesn't matter if her finger isn't bleeding. The Band-Aid means it is fixed. Bandages are cheap, and so are magic kisses.

There were some mixed feelings about the lake freezing. Some scientists were concerned that too much water was evaporating in previous winters and the lake's water levels had been consistently dropping. When the winter wind brought a sheet of ice to protect the lake, the scientists hoped the water levels would even out, or rise. Two hard winters have brought water levels up.

Bandages mean something.

So do the butterfly clips that fasten the wraps around chests. How they are named for an insect that must destroy itself in order to become.

It is possible to bind without bandages.

Clear plastic wrap also works, and it gives a little more than the medical wrap. I imagine it doesn't breathe well, skin to plastic, and would likely necessitate something between the two surfaces.

It is possible to not bind and still pass.

Two sports bras, a black t-shirt, and a flannel button down left unbuttoned paired with baggy jeans and hiking boots and it is possible to fool most people. Add a baseball cap and it is possible to go basically unnoticed.

I prefer to go unnoticed.

But sometimes it does not matter whether I am trying to disappear. Sometimes, despite every effort, the man on the street corner will yell to me, *Hey, sweetheart*. Or the flight attendant will say, *Anything for you, sir*? And more loudly just after, Oh I'm so sorry, ma'am. I am reminded I am not invisible.

Some things cannot be erased.

From the parking lot on the Island, I watch people in heavy jackets and heavy boots and fleece-lined deerskin hats and mittens walk out onto the frozen lake. They are black and green and hunter-orange twigs in the middle of an iced-over ocean. Giddy to be standing above 100 feet of blue-black water. Giddy to think about all the people and animals that used to stand here when the winters were colder more often. How wolves and moose crossed the miles of water from Canada to the Upper Peninsula and now they were standing on the lake. It is the surprise of the thing.

Officials try to warn residents of hollow spots and uneven freezing; crevasses that we think can only exist in Antarctica, or on mountains, and the officials remind us, no, there are 15-foot drops into water that hovers at freezing. It does little to deter people, so eager to get a new view of the world.

The bound body is a new view of self.

When I bound my breasts for the first time, I could not take my hands away from my chest, couldn't stop running my hands over the flat land that once held hills. For once I could not stop looking in the mirror. The novelty does not go away, I don't think—to see a body and recognize in the reflection a self that is truer than other selves and other bodies—it does not get less exciting.

Binding feels like new. Like bodies are made bright and shiny like pennies; our shirts button the way they are supposed to. We do not have to wear flannel like we are hiding something, even if we are hiding something.

But binding also feels like heavy wet snow packed on your chest. Not binding feels like that too, and I don't know how to clarify that the two feelings are exactly the same, and not.

The winter the lake freezes, I want out. I want to get away from the North, and the snow, and wind that makes my face hurt, and a monochrome landscape that sucks the joy out of me. It is the most painful winter I have in the Upper Peninsula, and I want it to be magical.

Binding is control. In things like gender, control over my own body is everything. Occasionally more important than basic needs when the anxiety about how a body looks and feels takes over. There is no saying when this will happen, or how to predict it. Body troubles are not specific to gender-benders, but it is a specific kind of body trouble that is different from mass-media pressures on bodies. It stems from the desire to pass and not pass at the same time. To fuck up perceptions of what it means to be a woman or man, to be everything in between all at once. It stems from a fear of fucking up the wrong person's perceptions at the wrong time on the wrong day. It only takes one person to follow me to my car, to pull me into an alley, to rape the masculine out of me, prove to me it really only requires the right man.

When the ice begins melting, I start seeing someone who binds and I do not want my body to be complicated. He binds his breasts as tight as he can, hikes up Sugarloaf, through the woods, up flight after flight of stairs to look out over the lake and icebergs. I do not ask him if he is okay with the trek. He would not complete it without his binder.

I do not want my body to be complicated. My binder does not fit properly, anyway, I say. It's okay, I say. And it is, because I really believe it is. And I put all my effort into being supportive and understanding and it feels nice to have someone sleep next to me.

So, it is okay because I say it is.

This is how coping works.

I'm not sure what I am coping with. Maybe it is Seasonal Affective Disorder. And dysphoria. And depression. And anxiety. And maybe all these things are one whole thing called something different. It all wraps around itself, wraps around me: an Ace bandage wrap.

It happens every year or so that when the ice goes out, people start jumping off Black Rocks on the north side of the Island too soon. The water takes a long time to warm up. The Coast Guard gets called at least once to rescue a swimmer in the too-cold water, and I imagine them: their lips blue, fingers numb, teeth chattering, lungs hiccupping for air as blood rushes to protect the heart and nothing else.

There is no control on the lake, even when I am looking for it. Even when it is frozen. Even when it looks solid and safe, if I sit long enough on Sunset Point, I can hear Superior groan as the ice shifts and grinds against itself and I know that the lake is only doing what it has done every year since it began.

With my mittened hands stuffed in my pockets, I shiver against the wind, just once. I take a deep breath, and remind myself it's not healthy for Superior to be bound up for too many months. The lake must thaw.

Acknowledgments

The hands that have held this collection—knowingly and unknowingly—are too many to count. But there are several people without whom this book would not exist.

Cornerstone Press: thank you for your time and careful attention to this collection and for shepherding it, and me, through the publishing process.

Jen Howard, Josh Anderson, and Matt Frank: thank you for believing in my writing before I did.

May-lee Chai, my fearless thesis chair: thank you for pushing me to not shy away from the hard things.

David Gessner: thank you for believing there's room and need for queer nature writing.

Mark Cox: thank you for assuring me that not-writing is as important as writing.

To my parents: thank you for knowing the value of art.

Zarah: thank you for poems and sound and looking at the world.

Megan: thank you for all those days in grad school when we weren't certain what this whole "writing thing" was for. Thank you for talking me through each one of these essays. For knowing what I wanted to say before I did.

Tyler: thank you for bringing me back to words. Again and again.

And to Lake Superior: thank you for being Home.

Gratefully acknowledged are the journals who gave these essays their first homes:

"Pulse" first appeared in *Ninth Letter*
"The Violence of Comets" first appeared as "Asteroid" in *|tap| lit mag*
"The Geography of Pronouns" first appeared in *Entropy*
"Picnic" first appeared in *Shenandoah Literary Journal*
"Siren Song" first appeared in *Orion*
"Bound Body" first appeared in *Fourth Genre*
"Empty the Land" first appeared in *Newfound*

MARTHA LUNDIN is a writer and educator living in Minnesota. They completed their MFA in nonfiction at the University of North Carolina, Wilmington. Martha's work can be found in *Fourth Genre, Newfound*, *Gertrude Press*, *Ninth Letter*, and *Shenandoah Literary Journal*, among others.

CPSIA information can be obtained
at www.ICGtesting.com
Printed in the USA
BVHW041650020622
638739BV00006B/184